AbraVocabra

The Amazingly Sensible Approach to Teaching Vocabulary

Amy Rider

Bonnie Benham
Dawn DiPrince
Stacy Hosek
Randy Larson
Susan Malmstadt
Cheryl Miller Thurston

Cottonwood Press, Inc.
Fort Collins, Colorado

Requests for permission should be addressed to:

Cottonwood Press, Inc.
305 West Magnolia, Suite 398
Fort Collins, CO 80521

ISBN 1-877673-32-3

Printed in the United States of America

Table of Contents

AbraVocabra Basics

Helping students improve their vocabularies is a project with enormous benefits. When students improve their vocabularies, they feel smarter. They find themselves understanding more of what they read and what they hear. They find it easier to express themselves because they have a better command of their language. They feel more powerful because, indeed, they are more powerful.

Luckily, vocabulary improvement is a relatively easy project for the classroom, and one that reaps results almost immediately. *AbraVocabra* makes vocabulary study easy, interesting, practical and, yes, even enjoyable!

The methods described in *AbraVocabra* are based on two fundamental ideas:

1. Vocabulary study should be based on common words, not obscure words that students will encounter only once or twice in a lifetime.
2. Vocabulary is not the same as spelling.

Common words. Vocabulary study is too often focused on unusual words encountered in novels, short stories or other materials students are reading in class. Just because the words "pasquinade" or "saloop" occur in a story doesn't mean that most people need to know them. Certainly, a teacher should point out the meanings in the context of the story, but having students memorize definitions of words they are unlikely to encounter again is a waste of time.

The words in AbraVocabra are real-world words, words that anyone is likely to read in a newspaper, hear on the news, read in a magazine. In fact, just seeing and hearing the words outside the classroom reinforces for students the idea that the words are useful and important ones to know.

Vocabulary vs. spelling. Too often, schools lump vocabulary and spelling together. On vocabulary tests, teachers require students to know the correct spelling, as well as the meaning, of the words.

The problem is that learning to spell and learning the meaning of a word are two different processes. You can learn to spell something without knowing its meaning, just as you can learn a word's meaning without having any idea how to spell it. That doesn't mean that knowing both isn't a good idea. It just means that one is neither dependent on nor necessary for the other.

Imagine teaching an auto repair class. If your goal is to teach auto repair, you probably aren't going to require students to spell every part of the engine correctly. Teaching spelling along with auto repair would only slow everyone down.

With vocabulary study, it is important to ask, "What am I trying to teach here, anyway? What is my goal?" If your goal is to help your students expand their vocabularies as much as possible, then it is not a good idea to require them to know how to spell each vocabulary word they learn.

Before English teachers everywhere have heart attacks at such heresy, a bit of clarification is in order. You should still *encourage* students to learn how to spell the words and, in fact, you should *require* correct spelling of the words whenever students use them. However, it is important to allow them to refer to the correct spelling, as needed. (With many students, just getting them to copy a word correctly is a big step in the right direction!)

Don't worry about parents or other teachers criticizing you for being too easy on the kids. You aren't being easy on them. Your goal is to build powerful vocabularies and to help your students expand their vocabularies as much as they possibly can. Teaching spelling will vastly slow down your progress. Explain your position. It is a perfectly justifiable one.

The truth is that people need to recognize and understand far more words than they ever need to be able to spell. If your goal is to help students learn as many new words as possible, take spelling out of the equation.

Using this book

AbraVocabra takes a practical approach to vocabulary study. Each of the 24 lists is made up of 10 practical words that anyone is likely to encounter in reading the newspaper, listening to the news or reading magazines. They are all useful words to know.

Students are not overwhelmed with long, impossible-looking lists. They receive 10 words at a time, with two bonus words thrown in. They study the words for 2-3 weeks at a time, using only a small amount of class time. If students study and learn all 24 lists over the course of a year, they will have learned 240 new words. Of course, you can easily do fewer lists, or even add your own words to the lists included in the book.

Here is the approach, in a nutshell, followed by a more detailed explanation of each step:

1. Have students guess the meaning of the words.
2. Have students "play" with the words, using them in a variety of activities.
3. Test students.
4. Review by playing Vocabra after every fourth set of words.

Have students guess the meaning of the words. Each word in an *AbraVocabra* list includes two "tip-off" sentences. The tip-off sentences show the words in context and include clues as to their meaning. Read these sentences aloud or put them on the chalkboard or overhead. (If you're particularly creative or simply enjoy the thrill of ad-libbing, make up your own sentences right on the spot instead.) Let students try to guess the meaning of each word and come up with a correct definition on their own.

This "figuring out" step is very important. It puts students in an active role rather than a passive one of sitting back and receiving the answers from you or mindlessly copying definitions they often don't understand from a dictionary.

Students need definitions that make sense to them. The lists in *AbraVocabra* include simple definitions to use as a guideline. However, it is important to remember that only one or two common definitions are included for each word. Students who become familiar with one meaning can later learn other meanings of a word.

The main purpose of the tip-off sentences is to give students a context for remembering words. It is also helpful to share stories or helpful hints. For example, one teacher always tells this story about the word "erroneous":

> *My college roommate Ruth was in a car accident. My boyfriend and I rushed to the hospital. The hospital staff wouldn't give information unless we were relatives, so my boyfriend quickly identified himself as Ruth's brother. Later, he was paged to sign some papers. Of course, he didn't want to sign papers, so he told the nurse, "I'm afraid you have received some erroneous information about my relationship to Ruth." The nurse looked at him blankly. "Huh?" He repeated himself. She looked at him blankly again. Finally, he realized that she didn't know what "erroneous" meant. "The information was false," he said. "There's a misunderstanding. I'm afraid I'm not Ruth's brother."*

After that story, virtually all the students remember the definition, especially when the teacher also points out that the word "error" is almost entirely imbedded in "erroneous." Giving the students a context for the words helps them learn the words easily.

Have students start "playing" with the words. Spend anywhere from one to four weeks working on a given list of words with your students. You shouldn't have to take much class time for this, but students won't mind the time you do spend. In fact, your students will probably find themselves enjoying vocabulary study. The chapter "Playing with Vocabulary Words" (page 11) in *AbraVocabra* contains dozens of activities to help students get involved with their vocabulary words and use them. Use one or more of these activities for each list of words.

Test the students. When it seems that students know the words, schedule a test. (A test is included after each word list.) The test itself will be an activity that helps reinforce the words. For most students, the test will be a positive experience, for they will know the words and do well. Each test requires students to use the words and encourages them to be creative in finding ways to incorporate the bonus words into the test stories.

Review. After every four lists, play the Vocabra Game with your students to review and reinforce the words they have learned. (See directions on pages 24–26.)

Addressing a Few Questions

Why aren't the words listed by grade level? How do I know where to start my students? The *AbraVocabra* word lists are not divided into "sixth grade words" or "ninth grade words." That's because useful words are just that — useful words. The words included in this book are words that any reasonably educated person is likely to know.

The word lists in *AbraVocabra* are very loosely arranged by difficulty, from easier to harder. What's easier or harder? That's a judgment call. There is no formula here, just common sense based on years of experience with young people.

How do you know where to start your students? Ask them. Pick a list that seems to be at about their level. Read the words, one word at a time, and have students show by a raise of their hands if they know the word. This shouldn't take more than five minutes. No, it won't be highly scientific and accurate. Yes, a few kids will probably lie and say they know words that they don't know, and some will pretend not to know words that they know perfectly well. Still, you will get an idea. Pick a list of words that most students don't know. Start there. (Try to start at the beginning of a set of four, so that you can use the Vocabra game included after each set.)

The truth is, for most groups sixth grade and up, you can start about anywhere and find that most students don't know more than half the words. (Don't be insulted if there is a word here and there that you don't know. All of us have gaps in our knowledge.)

What about the students who know most or all of the words? Students who know most of a word list can have a different challenge, still within the framework of the class. Challenge them to come up with their own individual lists of words, using books, magazines, newspapers and other people (including you) for ideas. These students can receive extra credit for being tested on the regular class list *and* their own list.

No, you don't need to write extra tests. Give the students a real challenge by having them complete the same test as the other students, then continuing the test story so that all of their personal vocabulary words are used in a way that shows their meaning. Students who already have strong vocabularies will usually enjoy the creativity involved in adapting the test for their own purposes.

Students with their own lists can do most of the same activities as the rest of the class, but using different words. (For group activities, have them stick with the standard class list. They may not want to be singled out.) Students who know most, but not all, of the words in a list should use substitutions for only the words they already know.

How do you keep students honest with all this? You can't. However, you can try appealing to the "best and honest" part of them by encouraging them to substitute words when they already know some of them on a list. Point out that, yes, anyone can take the easy route and study words he already knows. However, he will gain nothing. He will be wasting time and going nowhere. Sometimes appealing to the best in students has surprising results, especially with vocabulary. Students quickly sense for themselves the power of new words, the feeling of understanding more, of feeling smarter — and they plunge ahead with enthusiasm.

What if my students know what a word means but use it in a strange way?
Students don't usually start off doing anything perfectly, and that applies to using new words as well. When teaching vocabulary, think about the phases of learning involved in making a word part of your vocabulary. Think of concentric circles, like this:

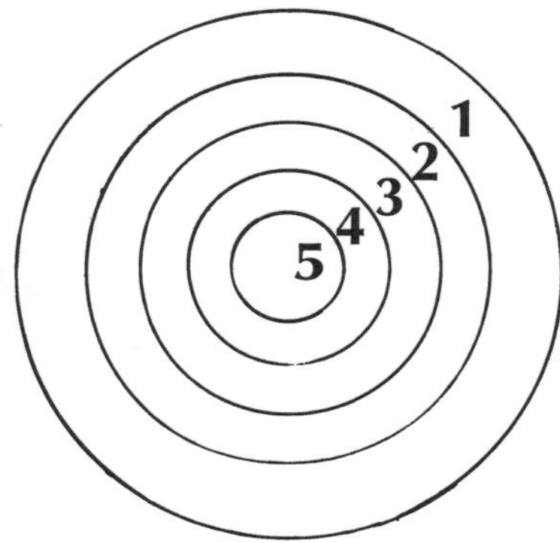

1. Noticing a word. Before you start to learn a word, you need to notice it. Quite often, the brain just skips over words that are unfamiliar.
2. Getting a general sense of the word's meaning. You may start recognizing that a word is generally positive or generally negative, or that it has something to do with astronomy, for example.
3. Getting a clearer sense of its meaning. The meaning becomes more sharply focused. While you still might not use the word yourself, you understand what it means, especially in context.
4. Being able to use the word in a way that is generally appropriate. When you first start using a new word, you may not use it quite correctly. You haven't learned the nuances of meaning, the prepositions usually associated with it, etc. However, you are getting there. (Little children may say "Want juice" before they learn to say, "I want some juice, please." That's okay. They don't have everything down pat, but that will come.)
5. Learning the subtleties of using the word correctly. More experience will lead to more appropriate use of the word. When you have learned the meaning of a word you will also, typically, start seeing it everywhere. Seeing it in other contexts will help you learn how to use the word appropriately.

Correct spelling of the word can occur at any of the five stages above — or not at all. Even people who can use a word correctly may still need to look it up in a the dictionary in order to spell it correctly.

Addressing a Few Questions

Does all this work? Yes. Here is what some teachers have said about the methods and ideas described in *AbraVocabra*:

- "My students started coming back to me after ninth grade achievement tests and saying, 'Hey, did you take our vocabulary words from the achievement tests? The tests were just full of them!' Well, of course I didn't. The words on the lists are just sensible words, and I suppose a lot of them may be on the achievement tests. I don't know. I do know that the kids were pretty pleased to feel so confident about how they did on at least one section of the test!"
- "After a few weeks of vocabulary study, my students always start saying, 'That word we learned is all over the place! I keep hearing it on TV and reading it in different places. How did you know it was going to start showing up everywhere?' I didn't know. It's just that once they learn a word, they start becoming aware of it. The word was appearing all along, but they didn't see it. Now that they know it, they are aware of it."
- "Vocabulary study has become such a positive thing in my classroom. When my principal observed me last year, my ninth graders were actually arguing about who should read his or her vocabulary story first. They were so excited, and my principal was impressed that I could get them excited about words."
- "I know our vocabulary study has been successful when my students start defining new vocabulary words with vocabulary words we have studied in the past. It always happens when I use this approach."
- "Vocabulary tests are something my kids actually look forward to! They all get a chance to do well, and the tests themselves often have them smiling and using their own creativity. Tests days are a real 'upper'!"

The key to learning new words is using them. Try some or all of the activity ideas that follow, choosing two or three activities for each word list. You don't need to spend a lot of time. You do need to get the students involved.

Playing with Vocabulary Words

As students do the various activities, take time to discuss how words can take different forms — for example, *scruples, scrupulous, unscrupulous* or *squalid* and *squalor.* As they come up, discuss word roots and their meanings and how they can help in figuring out the meaning of a word (Example: philo=love, anthro=man, philanthropist=a person who loves people and wants to increase their well-being, especially by charitable aid or donations).

The activities that follow are very successful in helping students learn new vocabulary words.

Story time

One of the most effective ways to get students to play with words is to have them put all the words in a vocabulary list into a story. This is a fairly sophisticated task, requiring students to understand the meanings of the words well enough to find a framework for them, thus relating all the words in some way.

Some students may not be able to do it. If they can't, allow them to use any "leftover" words in separate sentences that show their meaning. For young students, in fact, you may want to have them combine only two words at a time in a sentence or short paragraph.

Take time now and then to let students share their stories. They enjoy having an audience for their work, and some students will go to great lengths to create funny, entertaining stories — if they know their peers might hear them.

More challenges. Vary the story assignment in as many ways as possible. Give students some of these challenges, a different one each time:

- See how short you can make the story.
- Make the whole story about *one* of the following subjects: sports, cats or telephones.
- Write a story that includes *all* of the following subjects: sports, cats or telephones. Of course, you may use any other topics as well. See the following page for a few topic ideas for vocabulary stories.

  Possibilities for topics are endless. In fact, you might even want to have students write topic ideas on slips of paper. (Suggest that they choose interesting, specific nouns. "Pizza" is more interesting and specific than "food," for example.) Collect the slips of paper and put them in a jar. Then draw three topics for students to use in their stories. Save the jar and draw three different topics the next time you assign a story.

A few possible story topics:

fast food restaurants
football
MTV
the Internet
computers
skate boards
subways
pollution
sandals
parents
puppies
socks
CDs
teeth
birthdays
love
George Washington
lunch
volleyball
dragons
spinach
friends
cartoons
basketball
chocolate
Sunday
apples
mountains

grandparents
spiders
cars
vacations
in-line skates
extreme sports
boats
amusement park rides
movies
Egypt
kites
jeans
sisters
brothers
the Chicago Bulls
ice cream
broccoli
summer jobs
pizza
war
buffalo
tuna
lighthouses
spaghetti and meatballs
the alphabet
tricycles
Jell-O
the Grand Canyon

the Empire State Building
ferry boats
straws
coffee
colds
taxis
crayons
Darth Vader
video games
lacrosse
Will Smith
commercials
GI Joe dolls
tractors
lawn mowers
canned peaches
telephones
lime green
the Fourth of July
money
crushes
allergies
shopping
flutes
coconut cream pie
lockers
the Olympics
bouquet of roses

- One more idea is to have students write something other than a story, using the vocabulary words. Some examples: an acceptance speech, a lecture from a parent, a love letter, a commercial for a product, a letter of complaint or a newspaper article.

Grading tips: Vocabulary stories can be very easy to grade. Be sure to have students underline each word used. Then scan the stories quickly. If all the words are used in a sensible way, allow the full amount of points.

Another method is to assign two criteria for grading — for example, *using the vocabulary words correctly* and *having no run-on sentences*. Another time the criteria might be *using the vocabulary words correctly* and *having no spelling errors* (or no sentence fragments or no errors in capitalization or something else).

Choose a simple grading method that fits your style and your classroom. Don't turn the vocabulary stories into a huge pile of work for yourself. Just the act of doing the stories is the valuable part of the activity. In fact, sometimes you might not even want to grade the stories at all.

Oral Stories

A quick three to five minute lesson involves having students use the words orally. Have someone start a story, using as many words from the vocabulary list as possible in one minute. (Remind students that the story must indicate the word's meaning in some way.) Have someone else continue the story for a minute, and then someone else, for another minute. See how many words the class members can use, total, in three minutes.

Quickie Skits

Break the students into small groups of about five students each. Give the groups 10 minutes to come up with a short skit that uses as many vocabulary words as possible. (Of course, they act out the skits in front of the class.)

Acting Out the Meaning

At the end of class when you've got three minutes to spare, ask someone to volunteer to act out the meaning of a word. For example, someone might act out "rotund" by holding out her hands and imitating a round stomach.

Another idea is to give a volunteer (or volunteers) a situation to act out, using at least three vocabulary words in the performance. For example, you might give a student this situation to act out using the words "gawk," "grotesque" and "bicker": an irate customer talks to the stylist about her terrible hair cut.

A few more ideas for situations follow:

- At a supermarket, a chatty checker talks on and on and on.
- A convenience store manager hates kids and starts trying to get a group of them to leave the second they come into the store.
- An enthusiastic coach encourages her team.
- A teenager talks on the phone to her best friend.
- A parent lectures his son, who has come home five hours late.
- A mother can't get her baby to stop crying.
- A school bus breaks down five miles from school.
- A singer loses his voice during a performance.
- Two best friends say goodbye because one is moving away.
- A candidate running for office promises a free car to all sixteen-year-olds.

- Two business owners discuss ways to promote their bowling alley.
- Ice skaters arrive at a pond, only to find that the ice has melted.
- Three people on a diet decide what to have for lunch.
- Picnickers are plagued by ants.
- Three friends decide to start their own band.
- A student is afraid to show her parents her report card.
- A father drags his seven-year-old to the dentist.
- Parents explain to their children that the family won't be going to Disney World after all.
- A gardener shows off the 35-pound cantaloupe she grew in her garden.
- A ten-year-old finds a wallet full of hundred dollar bills.
- Three young people discover a time machine.
- A rock star performs before a huge audience, but the audience is not pleased.
- A waiter at a restaurant brings an irritable customer the wrong plate of food.
- A car stalls at a stop sign, and frustrated drivers are trapped in their car for eight blocks.
- Two actors try to do a commercial for "Zippy Dippy Drink," which they discover is an awful-tasting combination of carrot and spinach juice.

Drawing

See if students can draw the meaning of a word, using the word itself. Have them open their minds to all kinds of possibilities. Here are a couple of examples:

rotund

rOtund

macabre

MACABRE

Another idea is to assign a specific vocabulary word to each student. Then ask students to draw a picture that somehow illustrates their word, but without using the word itself in the illustration. (For example, a student might illustrate "gawk" by drawing someone with her eyeballs bulging.) The class as a whole then tries to guess which vocabulary word is illustrated by each picture.

Vocabulary Bee

To review words, have a vocabulary bee, conducted somewhat like a spelling bee. In a vocabulary bee, the class is divided into two teams. Unlike a spelling bee, however, students aren't eliminated from the game when they miss a word.

Because students will probably know most of the words, it's a good idea to add question "levels," to make the game more interesting. Let each student select a one, two or three point question. For one-point questions, students simply define the word correctly and earn their team a point. For two-point questions, they must define the word correctly and use it in a sentence. Three point questions require the student to define two words correctly and use both in one sentence that indicates their meaning.

Categories

After your class has studied four or five word lists, have students work in small groups to categorize the words, placing at least three words in each category. Students should come up with their own categories.

There are, of course, no limits to the number and kind of categories students might choose. Just a few examples: "adjectives," "words that begin with *t*," "words that describe someone who is mad," "words good for describing food," "words that would be perfect for a horror story," "three-letter words," "words used to describe someone negatively," "words that might be used by a doctor," etc.

Try not to give the groups any hints. Insist that the students themselves determine the categories, and remind them that there is no one right answer to the exercise. As long as the category has at least three words and the words fit the category, the answer is correct.

This exercise really requires creative thinking and a strong understanding of the words. It is an excellent activity for review.

A Novel Approach

Ask students to apply their vocabulary words to a novel (or short story) they are reading in class. A few examples: Moby Dick was a whale of *gargantuan* proportions. Daisy Miller was a *vivacious* young woman who was always into one thing or another. Miss Havisham was a *haughty* woman whom no one liked.

Journal Topics

If your students keep class journals, have them pick words from the vocabulary list that definitely *do* and definitely *do not* describe themselves. Ask them to elaborate.

Sell It

Divide the class into small groups, and give each group one of the assigned vocabulary words. Ask the group to imagine being an ad agency hired to sell the word to the rest of the class. Give students a short time to come up with an idea for a commercial or an advertisement that will show the word's usefulness and meaning.

Dialogue

Ask students to write a short two or three-person dialogue (conversation) using all the words on the vocabulary list. Or have them design a short comic strip that includes all the words. (The dialogue, of course, goes in the "bubbles.")

Newspaper Captions

Cut out several newspaper or magazine photographs. Ask students to come up with captions that include the vocabulary words and describe what might be happening in each photograph.

Write a Poem

Challenge students to write a short, two to four line rhyming poem for each word. Example:

Mom was indignant.
My father was mad.
I got grounded,
and I was sad.

Song Titles

Have students write titles of songs, movies, TV shows and/or books that include one or more of their vocabulary words. Some examples:

- "I Was *Indignant,* so I Ran Over His Lawn Mower With My Truck" — a country-western song
- *The Indignant Princess: A Story of Revenge* — a book

Sports Reports

Have students act as sports reporters, covering a sporting event of their choice. Each story should include all the vocabulary words. (Or allow students to write two or three short sports stories in order to use all the words.)

Setting up a Bonus System

Making vocabulary study — except for tests — an "extra" or a "bonus" often brings amazing results. Students who don't care much about doing the required work will work very hard for anything labeled "bonus." The system described below can have very positive results.

This bonus point system involves keeping a running total of bonus points on a chart for each class. Announce that whenever the bonus points reach a certain amount (say 300 or 500 points), the class will have a game day, with prizes. (See pages 18–21 for a game that works very well for game days. The games require thinking and involve words. Most kids enjoy them.)

Explain that bonus points are arbitrary, given and taken away according to your judgment or even your whim. You might give five bonus points one day for having someone define a word correctly. You might take two away another day because three students kept shouting out answers. Explain that you are the bonus point queen, king, dictator — whatever term you can dream up to fit. Do this with good humor, and keep it light. Don't turn bonus points into something that seems too much like grades.

Be free with your bonus points, and vary the amount you grant. Here are just a few ideas for using them:

- Take three minutes at the beginning of class and give a bonus point for each correct definition given as you call on different students. (You might even want to set a timer.)
- Another day, announce that you will give 10 class bonus points for anyone who can define all 10 vocabulary words, quickly. Ask for volunteers, or call on someone.
- Give two points to each student who uses a designated vocabulary word correctly in a sentence that shows the word's meaning. You might do two or three words at the beginning or end of class each day.
- Make students aware that you will give bonus points at any time, even out of the classroom. Call on students in the halls. Arrange for the principal to call a student to the office during homeroom and ask him what "homogenous" means. During an assembly, announce that you will give 10 bonus points to your third period English class if Alfred can define "infinitesimal." (Be sure to choose someone who can take the heat.)
- Tell kids you will take five minutes every now and then for reporting on "word sightings." If Dan Rather says "indignant" on the nightly news, give two points to the student who reports as much. If someone brings in a newspaper article with "erroneous" in it, allow a point or two.
- Make the point-giving truly subjective and random. Some days, if you are feeling generous, give 25 points for a simple question. On another day, give one point for a fairly hard question.
- With each test, keep a record of words that everyone in the class got right. Hang this list of words that your class "owns" on the wall and add to it each week. Give five bonus points for every "owned" word.
- Tell students that bonus points are just that — bonus. You can give them or take them away. If someone wants to argue loudly about something and disrupt the class, just quietly take away two points, then — if necessary — another two. You don't have to say much. Students will get the point. Best of all, they won't usually support the student who is disruptive. Handled lightly and with good humor, this technique can help your students behave, as well as help them learn vocabulary.
- The following games (pages 18–21) make an excellent reward for students earning enough bonus points for a game day.

Name ______________________________

For each category listed along the left side of the page, think of an appropriate word that begins with the letter at the top of the column. The first item is done for you.

	V	O	C	A	B	U	L	A	R	Y
Items of clothing	*vests*									
Things you might find in a kitchen										
6-letter words										
Names of TV shows										
Things at a wedding										

Name ______________________________

For each category listed along the left side of the page, think of an appropriate word that begins with the letter at the top of the column. The first item is done for you.

	V	O	C	A	B	U	L	A	R	Y
Things advertised in commercials	*Vaseline*									
Sandwich ingredients										
Things that fly										
Items of furniture										
Words that are related to sports										

Name ______________________________

For each category listed along the left side of the page, think of an appropriate word that begins with the letter at the top of the column. The first item is done for you.

	V	O	C	A	B	U	L	A	R	Y
Colors	*violet*									
Girls' names										
Parts of an automobile										
5-letter adjectives										
Kinds of candy										

Name ______________________________

For each category listed along the left side of the page, think of an appropriate word that begins with the letter at the top of the column. The first item is done for you.

	Things that can make a teacher irate	Verbs with 5 or more letters	Famous people from history (last names)	Careers and jobs	Something a person can usually get at a shop-ping mall
V	*vandal-ized desks*				
O					
C					
A					
B					
U					
L					
A					
R					
Y					

Possible answers to bonus games:

	V	O	C	A	B	U	L	A	R	Y
Items of clothing	*vests*	*overcoat*	*cap*	*anorak*	*blazer*	*under-wear*	*leotard*	*anklets*	*romper*	*yar-mulke*
Things you might find in a kitchen	*vitamins*	*oven mitt*	*Cuisin-art*	*apples*	*bowls*	*utensils*	*lemon*	*after-dinner mints*	*refriger-ator*	*yams*
6-letter words	*viking*	*orange*	*colors*	*animal*	*banana*	*urgent*	*lounge*	*aspens*	*runner*	*yellow*
Names of TV shows	*Victory at Sea*	*Oprah*	*Coach*	*Actual Stories of the Highway Patrol*	*Blossom*	*Unsolved Mysteries*	*Laugh-In*	*Andy Griffith Show*	*Ricki Lake*	*Young and the Restless*
Things at a wedding	*veil*	*organdy*	*candle*	*atten-dants*	*bride*	*usher*	*lace*	*altar*	*roses*	*yummy food*

	V	O	C	A	B	U	L	A	R	Y
Things adver-tised in com-mercials	*Vaseline*	*orange juice*	*Chevy trucks*	*AT&T*	*beer*	*under-wear*	*laundry deter-gent*	*Alaska*	*restau-rants*	*yogurt*
Sandwich ingredients	*vinegar*	*onion*	*crusty French bread*	*alfalfa sprouts*	*butter*	*Under-wood ham*	*lettuce*	*avocado*	*radish*	*yellow mustard*
Things that fly	*vampire bat*	*oriole*	*condor*	*alba-tross*	*B52 bomber*	*UFO*	*Learjet*	*airplane*	*rocket*	*yellow jacket*
Items of furniture	*valet*	*ottoman*	*cabinet*	*arm-chair*	*buffet*	*utility table*	*lounge chair*	*armoire*	*rocking chair*	*youth bed*
Words that are related to sports	*volley*	*out-of-bounds*	*clipping*	*ace*	*bases*	*uniform*	*lob*	*athlete*	*run*	*yell*

	V	O	C	A	B	U	L	A	R	Y
Colors	*violet*	*orange*	*cream*	*apple red*	*blue*	*umber*	*lime*	*auber-gine*	*rose*	*yellow*
Girls' names	*Veronica*	*Opal*	*Connie*	*Amy*	*Brenda*	*Ursula*	*Linda*	*Allison*	*Rhonda*	*Yolanda*
Parts of an automobile	*valve*	*odome-ter*	*cam-shaft*	*air filter*	*bolts*	*under-carriage*	*lights*	*air con-ditioner*	*rotor*	*yoke*
5-letter adjectives	*valid*	*obese*	*crude*	*acute*	*brisk*	*upper*	*loose*	*angry*	*rowdy*	*young*
Kinds of candy	*vanilla taffy*	*O'Henry*	*carmel*	*Altoids*	*Big Hunk*	*U-No Bars*	*Laffy Taffy*	*Almond Joy*	*Reese's*	*York Pep-permint Patties*

	V	O	C	A	B	U	L	A	R	Y
Things that can make a teacher irate	*vandal-ized desks*	*obnox-ious behavior*	*cheating*	*armpit noises*	*bullies*	*unsatis-factory work*	*lewd behavior*	*absent students*	*rowdy students*	*yelling in class*
Verbs with 5 or more letters	*vocalize*	*ostracize*	*careen*	*amble*	*break*	*utilize*	*languish*	*attack*	*reign*	*yodel*
Famous people from history (last names)	*Voltaire*	*Jackie Kennedy Onassis*	*Jimmy Carter*	*John Quincy Adams*	*John Wilkes Booth*	*Pope Urban II*	*Abe Lincoln*	*Crispus Attucks*	*Paul Revere*	*Brigham Young*
Careers and jobs	*vice-princi-pal*	*oil baron*	*curator*	*astro-physicist*	*boxing champ*	*under-taker*	*lab assistant*	*architect*	*rock star*	*yeoman*
Something a person can usually get at a shopping mall	*videos*	*Orange Julius*	*CDs*	*artwork*	*bargains*	*under-wear*	*lotion*	*anklets*	*running shoes*	*Yankees' hat*

Directions to Vocabra Game

Overview

With Vocabra, teams compete against each other to define vocabulary words correctly. They earn or lose points, according to point values they themselves decide to risk for each round. Words are selected through random drawings, so students never know which words they will be asked to define.

The teams consist of two student teams and a third "team" made up of just the teacher. It is possible for either student team *or* the teacher to win the game. Of course, the finer points of the game help make it more interesting. These are outlined below.

Preparation

1. There is a Vocabra game card located after every fourth word list. Photocopy the card containing the words your class is currently studying. Make a transparency of it for the overhead projector. (It is also possible to draw the game card on the chalk board, if you don't have access to an overhead. Another possibility is to photocopy the game card and give each student a copy.)
2. Photocopy page 161 and cut apart the numbers and letters on the copy. Put the number slips in a "number jar" and the letter slips in a "letter jar." (Okay, it could also be a box. Or a paper bag. Or a sock.) Note that "A1" and "A2" refer to the first and second "A"s that spell out "Vocabra" on the cards.
3. Have a clock, timer or watch readily accessible.
4. Divide the class into two equally sized teams and have the teams sit on separate sides of the room. Determine a "play order" for each team — usually left to right, or front to back along the rows.
5. Draw three columns on the chalkboard for recording scores. Head two of the columns with the teams' names (or Team A, Team B). Head the third column "Teacher."

Playing the Game

1. Explain that, once play begins, the game will continue for exactly 30 minutes. When the timer sounds, the game is over, no matter what is happening at that time. The team with the most points at that time is the winner. Point out that either team or you, the teacher, can be the winner of the game. (In fact, it's fun to make an agreement ahead of time about the prizes for the winners. As the teacher, you can have some fun with what your prize might be. Be creative!)
2. Give a brief overview of the game: Vocabra is played in rounds. A "risk taker" from one team decides how many points he is going to risk (from 5–50 points, in increments of 5), without knowing which word on the game board he will be asked to define. If he defines the word correctly, his team will earn the amount of points he has risked. If he

misses the word, his team will lose the amount of points he has risked, and the opposing team will have a chance to define the word and earn the points. If both teams miss the word, the teacher gets the points. (That's how the teacher earns points — when neither team can define a word.) The next round begins with a risk taker from the other team.

Point out that you, the teacher, will make the final determination on the correctness of a definition. Explain that you are looking for reasonably clear explanations of what a word means, not dictionary definitions. If a student's definition is not quite clear enough, though not *wrong*, you may ask her to use it in a sentence, for clarification.

Also point out that the rules of Vocabra give the teacher another power: subtracting points for excessive rowdiness or rudeness (five points at a time works well) and for shouting out the correct definition to a word. Explain that you will not award points when someone on a team shouts the definition to the risk taker.

Example. Assume that you have flipped a coin and determined that Team A will play first. The first risk taker in the play order for that team is Joe, who decides to risk 25 points.

A member of the other team then draws a slip from the letter jar and a slip from the number jar — in this case a C and a 8. That means the location of Joe's word is C-8 on the Vocabra Card. The teams are using the first Vocabra Card on page 49, so Joe's word is *egotistical*. (Note: After being drawn, the slips go back in the number and letter jars. In future rounds, it's possible that C and 8 can be drawn again.)

Joe then has 30 seconds to give an accurate definition of *egotistical*. If he does so, his team earns 25 points. If he can't do so, his team loses 25 points. (Yes, negative scores are possible.) Play then goes to Team B, and the next person on Team B gets a chance at defining the word. If she defines *egotistical* correctly, her team earns 25 points. If she misses it, however, her team does *not* lose points. (After all, her team didn't decide how much to risk.) Instead, the 25 points go to the teacher.

After the points risked have been recorded on the chalk board (whether to Team A, Team B or the teacher), the next round begins with Team B, even though a Team B player had the last chance at a definition. That's because the initial risk taker for each round alternates between Team A and Team B.

3. Some of the factors that make the game interesting are these:
   - Along with the regular vocabulary words, bonus words appear on each Vocabra card, as well as eight "weird words" — words that are unusual or strange-sounding and not widely known. Students need to remember, when they choose the number of points they will risk, that they might wind up with *any* of these words.
   - When neither team knows the definition of a word, the teacher gives the definition (The definitions for the "weird words" appear in the Appendix, page 162.) Students are advised to pay attention because the same word could come up again.

- Risk takers are, in a sense, "betting" on the likelihood that they will know a word. It is important for them to remember that they can *lose* points for their teams as well as gain points.
- Chance plays a big part in the game. Words are selected at random, by drawing the number and letter slips from the jars. Sometimes the "weird words" will come up again and again. Sometimes they won't be selected at all. No one knows what words will be selected in a drawing.

One final note: Have fun with Vocabra. The point is to help students review and reinforce the words they have learned. The atmosphere should be one of light-hearted competition and risk taking. Take a playful attitude, not a deadly serious one. Enjoy your students. Enjoy the review!

AbraVocabra Word Lists 1–24

Vocabulary List #1

annual: happening once a year

- The clothing store holds an **annual** back-to-school sale every September.
- "My dad makes more money **annually** than your dad," Percy bragged.

grotesque: weird; distorted

- The costume store had a lot of really **grotesque** masks. Julie wanted the one of the zombie with acid on its face.
- When Marco looked at the **grotesque** angle of his arm, he knew it had to be broken.

gawk: to stare stupidly

- Kendra and Jessica **gawked** at Brad Pitt when he entered the elevator with them.
- Matthew was **gawking** at the New York skyscrapers when he stepped into an open manhole and broke his leg.

obese: very fat

- Eddie Murphy plays an **obese** man in *The Nutty Professor*.
- The health teacher blames potato chips and afternoon TV for so many of today's young people being **obese**.

toxic: poisonous; unhealthy; harmful

- In the movie, *Batman*, the Joker fell into a large vat of **toxic** green stuff that melted his skin.
- Be careful when eating wild mushrooms. Some of them are **toxic** and may harm you.

blunder: a stupid or clumsy mistake

- The TV show "The Fresh Prince of Bel Air" usually ends with footage of all the **blunders** the actors made while rehearsing.
- Nobody's perfect. Everyone makes a **blunder** every once in a while.

bicker: to fight or quarrel over something silly

- The children **bickered** over the cupcake until their mother got so irritated she took it away, and neither child got any.
- Even though he felt it was unfair, Lucas refused to **bicker** with his English teacher about his test grade.

brutal: vicious; cruel

- Southern Californians may never understand how people can survive the **brutal** cold and heavy snow of Minnesota winters.
- After the **brutal** soccer match, Joanna was bruised and sore.

feline: cat-like; a member of the cat family

- The dog preferred **feline** food to its own Puppy Chow.
- When they lost a second **feline** to leukemia, the Wanners decided not to get any more pets.

tyrant: a ruler who abuses power

- When Charlie is put in charge of his younger sisters and brothers, he often behaves like a **tyrant**.
- "My dad is a **tyrant**," grumbled Ross. "His word is law in our house."

Bonus Words

★dumbfounded: speechless because of shock or amazement

- Because the lottery winner was **dumbfounded**, the reporters couldn't get a direct quote from her.
- Cherisse was **dumbfounded** when she discovered someone had painted her Volkswagen purple and green.

★waiver: a document that shows a person voluntarily gives up a right, claim or privilege

- Tawnie signed a **waiver** of her right to an attorney. She wanted to represent herself in court.
- Patricia's **waiver** of parental guardianship made adoption of her child much easier for the Edmonds.

Name ______________________________

Test

Matching

Match each word in the left column to its correct definition in the right column.

____ 1. bicker
____ 2. tyrant
____ 3. feline
____ 4. annual
____ 5. gawk
____ 6. brutal
____ 7. toxic
____ 8. obese
____ 9. grotesque
____ 10. blunder

★Bonus words

____ 11. waiver
____ 12. dumbfounded

a. happening once a year
b. very fat
c. very blonde
d. vicious; cruel
e. a document that shows a person voluntarily gives up a right, claim or privilege
f. weird; distorted
g. to fight or quarrel over something silly
h. a stupid or clumsy mistake
i. poisonous; unhealthy; harmful
j. a ruler who abuses power
k. to stare stupidly
l. cat-like; a member of the cat family
m. armadillo-like; a member of the armadillo family
n. speechless because of shock or amazement
o. cheesy

Fill-in-the-Blank

Directions: The first 10 words listed above belong in the story below. Read the story and use the clues in the text to place each word in the correct blank space provided. You may change the form of a word to fit the story, if you need to. (For example, you might need to add *ed*, *ing*, *ly* or *s*.)

Killer Kitty

Jason couldn't believe his eyes. He (1)________________ at the blubbery mound in the alley. He'd never seen such an (2)______________ animal before in his life. What was a baby walrus doing in the alley behind his house? Then it hit him — it wasn't a walrus at all. It was a giant furry (3)_____________ that must have weighed at least 25 pounds!

List #1 continued

"That's not a cat, you dimwit," grumbled his brother Scott. Scott was a year older and bigger than Jason, and he thought everything that Jason did or said was wrong or stupid. "Cats are prissy, fluffy little things that play with balls of yarn. That (4)_______________ thing is ragged and matted and looks like an old rug someone threw out. You're always making stupid (5)_______________ like this," Scott said. "Go back in the house right now before I feed you to this thing."

Scott's last comment didn't scare Jason. Scott always tried to act like a (6)_______________, but by now Jason was smart enough to know when Scott's threats were empty. "Look," Jason said. "It's got whiskers and a long tail, and it's shedding, which is why it looks so awful. It is a cat."

"It is not!"

"Is too!" Jason hated (7)_______________ with his brother, but what else could he do? Big brothers were pretty much a pain in the neck.

"It looks like it fell into that pit full of (8)_______________ waste down by the factory," he continued. "The factory had its (9)_______________ drain and pipe cleaning a few days ago. The cat must have fallen into the pit, and the chemicals probably ate away part of its fur."

"Oh yeah?" said Scott. "I'll prove to you that it's not a cat. I'll go over and take a closer look."

"I wouldn't do that if I were you," Jason warned. "It doesn't look too friendly."

"Oh, you're nothing but a big chicken. Let your big brother take care of it for you."

Scott headed toward the large blob. Just as he was about to touch it, the blob sprang into the air and sank its claws into Scott's jeans. Scott let out a scream and tried to shake the cat off, but the cat held on for dear life. After a (10)_______________ assault on Scott's now bloody leg, the cat finally released Scott from its grip and took off. Scott limped back toward Jason, muttering not-very-kind comments about the "stupid cat." His face was very red.

Jason looked at his angry brother and smiled to himself. "I could get to love a cat like that one!"

Super Challenge

Directions: Use the bonus words from the list on the test to finish the story above.

Vocabulary List #2

fragile: easily broken

- Mrs. Malmo put away all her **fragile** glass knickknacks whenever her one-year-old grandson came to visit.
- Raw eggs are more **fragile** than hard-boiled ones.

vast: very large

- Because Professor Montoya had been to almost every country in the world, she had a **vast** knowledge of many different cultures.
- Although she had a **vast** collection of sweaters in her closet, Joyce couldn't find one to match her green jeans.

swagger: a strut; to walk or conduct yourself in a bragging, conceited way

- To make his character seem boastful and confident, the actor **swaggered** onto the stage.
- Television characters Fonzie and Vinnie Barbarino are both known for their cool **swagger** on reruns of "Happy Days" and "Welcome Back, Kotter."

vivid: lively; bright; full of life or color

- Savannah can't read horror stories because with such a **vivid** imagination, the stories seem real to her.
- The colors in the painting were so **vivid** they seemed to jump out at anyone walking into the room.

soothe: to calm or relieve

- When Richard has nightmares, the only thing that **soothes** his fears is having his cat come sleep with him.
- A good hypnotist can **soothe** you in minutes, using only her voice.

glutton: someone who eats or consumes an amazing amount

- John is a **glutton** when it comes to ice cream. He can eat a gallon at a time.
- "Nadia is now such a **glutton** that we have to order three pizzas just to feed the two of us," complained the husband of the mother-to-be.

irate: very angry

- The teacher was **irate** when not one student turned in the homework she had assigned the day before.
- Britta's dad was worried and also **irate** when she forgot to call home.

prompt: on time; done without delay

- "**Prompt** return of your library books is appreciated," said the librarian. "Those who turn their books in late will have to pay a fine."
- Emily never keeps people waiting. She is very **prompt**.

dictator: a ruler with absolute power and authority

- If he does not abuse his power, a **dictator** is not a tyrant.
- "Mr. Collins is a **dictator** in his classroom," said Madison. "Nobody can take a breath without his permission."

intoxicated: drunk; exhilarated

- It is a crime to drive a car while **intoxicated**.
- The fragrance of the flowers was so **intoxicating** it made Carmen feel dizzy.

Bonus Words

★palatial: suitable for a palace or palace-like

- "Marble floors and gold light fixtures!" gasped Joe. "Isn't this rather **palatial** for a garage?"
- With his lottery winnings, Mr. Braden bought 25 acres and created **palatial** gardens that were a sight to behold.

★omen: a sign or warning of things to come

- Sneaking into her house an hour after curfew, Kelsey heard a dog bark and knew it was a bad **omen**. Then she saw her parents' light switch on.
- Mary wondered if her dream about passing her driver's license test was a good **omen**.

Name ______________________________

Test

Matching

Match each word in the left column to its correct definition in the right column.

____ 1. dictator
____ 2. soothe
____ 3. fragile
____ 4. vivid
____ 5. prompt
____ 6. intoxicated
____ 7. glutton
____ 8. swagger
____ 9. irate
____ 10. vast

★**Bonus words**
____ 11. palatial
____ 12. omen

a. very large
b. very angry
c. very ugly
d. a strut; to walk or conduct yourself in a bragging, conceited way
e. suitable for a palace or palace-like
f. lively; bright; full of life or color
g. to calm or relieve
h. a kind of crown worn by beauty contestants
i. a sign or warning of things to come
j. someone who eats or consumes an amazing amount
k. easily broken
l. drunk; exhilarated
m. on time; done without delay
n. a ruler with absolute power and authority
o. a yardstick with absolute power and authority

Fill-in-the-Blank

Directions: The first 10 words listed above belong in the story below. Read the story and use the clues in the text to place each word in the correct blank space provided. You may change the form of a word to fit the story, if you need to. (For example, you might need to add *ed*, *ing*, *ly* or *s*.)

Enchilada Supreme

Wanda was always (1)________________ when she returned home from her job at the Burrito Barn. Almost before she got through the door, she was ranting and raving about Skip, her pasty-faced manager. He had a (2)________________ number of faults, not the least of which was his tendency to say "uh" every 15 seconds or so. He drove Wanda crazy.

Wanda's family loved her and hated to hear her complain, so they tried anything and everything to (3)________________ the poor girl. But when nothing, not even dimming the lights and playing New Age guitar music, could calm Wanda down, Wanda's mother begged her to quit the Burrito Barn and find a new job.

However, Wanda couldn't bring herself to quit because that meant she would lose her employee discount on the Burrito Barn's Enchilada Supreme. She loved the Supreme more than any other food in the world. She was such a (4)________________ when it came to those enchiladas that nothing, not even Skip, could make her quit her job.

One Saturday evening in March, Wanda's family listened wearily to more of her complaints about Skip, whom she now referred to as "the (5)______________" because of his new rule that every Burrito Barn employee must wear a Beanie Burrito hat. "Since he made that new rule," Wanda continued, "Skip's been worse than ever. Plus, the guy seems to have this idea that he is so cool. He (6)_______________ around the restaurant, running his fingers through that gross Elvis Presley wave in his hair and not looking where he is going. He's so clumsy, though, that instead of looking cool, he looks (7)________________, stumbling around like he's had too much to drink."

Finally Wanda's family had had enough. To get her to leave the Burrito Barn, they decided to give her nothing for breakfast, lunch and dinner except the Burrito Barn's Enchilada Supreme.

At first they thought their plan had backfired. Wanda seemed delighted to eat enchiladas three times a day. But after two and a half weeks, her attitude had changed. She was so disgusted by the Enchilada Supreme that she never wanted to see the Burrito Barn again.

The next morning, Wanda reported to work (8)________________ at 11:00 AM, planning to turn in her resignation. Before she could even open her mouth, though, Skip yelled at her for mixing Monterey Jack cheese with cheddar the night before. Without taking a breath, he went on and on and on. Finally, to get his attention, Wanda marched right up to him with the Super Sour Cream Shooter. Aiming at his lime green Burrito Barn polo shirt, she wrote her resignation in sour cream. Skip, who was really insecure at heart and had a (9)_______________ ego, blushed a (10)________________ shade of red and began to cry. Wanda felt sorry for him, but she had had enough. She walked out of the Burrito Barn and tossed her Beanie Burrito hat into the Dumpster.

Super Challenge

Directions: Use the bonus words from the list on the test to finish the story above.

____

____

____

____

____

____

____

____

____

____

____

____

Vocabulary List #3

immortal: living forever; indestructible

- Lamar never wears his seat belt when he's in a car, and he never wears his helmet when he rides a bike. He must think he's **immortal** or something.
- When Mike survived a thirty-foot fall from a building, some people were so amazed that they thought he might be **immortal**.

pessimistic: feeling gloomy and hopeless; thinking the worst

- Ruthie was so **pessimistic**. She was just sure she would lose the student council race, get an *F* in algebra and not make the basketball team.
- Oscar says his belief that the world will soon end is realistic, not **pessimistic**.

barbaric: uncivilized; wild; crude

- Many people think that grounding is a **barbaric** form of punishment. These people are usually teenagers.
- The speaker shouted, "If we want to call ourselves a civilized society, this **barbaric** violence has got to stop."

tragic: disastrous; bringing great harm and suffering

- The tanker spilled several million gallons of oil into the sea. The **tragic** event left over 300 animals dead along the shore.
- Cynthia cried and carried on as though getting a flat bicycle tire was the most **tragic** thing in the world.

sulk: to mope around or pout

- Joe sat on the sofa frowning and refusing to talk to anyone after he failed his driver's test. "Are you going to **sulk** all night or start studying?" asked his father.
- The second grader was **sulking** in the hallway after being sent to the principal's office.

compassion: sympathy; pity; concern

- We should show caring and **compassion** for those less fortunate than us.
- "If you want to show **compassion** for the homeless," said Megan, "donate food and clothing to a homeless shelter."

mortal: a being that must eventually die; deadly; fatal

- "Unlike video game characters, who seem to live forever, humans are **mortal** beings," Bobby's mother reminded him.
- The little bear cub received a **mortal** wound. He stopped breathing before the hunter put his gun down.

recoil: to draw back because of fear, surprise or disgust

- Paul **recoiled** when he opened the barn door and saw a rattlesnake.
- Tia's cat is brave, but even it **recoiled** when the rabid raccoon attacked.

optimistic: hopeful; looking on the bright side

- **Optimistic** that he would win the election, the politician bought a new suit and tie especially for his victory party.
- Since Sally studied three hours for her algebra final, she was **optimistic** that she would pass it.

vain: conceited; having a high opinion of oneself

- Quincy is so **vain** he can hardly tear himself away from his mirror.
- Marie is **vain** about her beautiful black hair. She brushes it all the time.

Bonus Words

★gargantuan: huge; gigantic

- Timmy picked out a **gargantuan** Christmas tree, but his mother said they would never find enough ornaments to cover it.
- Jake's Aunt Gladys has a **gargantuan** beehive hairdo that makes her look a foot taller than she really is.

★hoodwink: to trick, confuse or deceive

- Ferris **hoodwinked** his parents into believing he was sick by heating up his forehead with the electric heating pad.
- The little girl was **hoodwinked** by her older brother into cleaning her room. "If you don't clean it, Santa Claus will fill your stocking with pebbles and grass clippings," he said.

Name ______________________________

Test

Matching

Match each word in the left column to its correct definition in the right column.

____ 1. compassion
____ 2. vain
____ 3. pessimistic
____ 4. barbaric
____ 5. tragic
____ 6. immortal
____ 7. sulk
____ 8. mortal
____ 9. optimistic
____ 10. recoil

★Bonus Words

____ 11. gargantuan
____ 12. hoodwink

a. feeling gloomy and hopeless; thinking the worst
b. uncivilized; wild; crude
c. conceited; having a high opinion of oneself
d. disastrous; bringing great harm and suffering
e. to trick, confuse or deceive
f. to mope around or pout
g. to mop around a piece of furniture
h. sympathy; pity; concern
i. a being that must eventually die; deadly; fatal
j. to draw back because of fear, surprise or disgust
k. to draw a picture because of an art class assignment
l. hopeful; looking on the bright side
m. living forever; indestructible
n. huge, gigantic
o. a kind of after shock following an earthquake

Fill-in-the-Blank

Directions: The first 10 words listed above belong in the story below. Read the story and use the clues in the text to place each word in the correct blank space provided. You may change the form of a word to fit the story, if you need to. (For example, you might need to add *ed*, *ing*, *ly* or *s*.)

Roommates

Once upon a time, two trolls lived together in a tree trunk. The roommates were woodland creatures and had no furniture, dishes or towels. They ate with their hands, slept on the ground and, all in all, lived a rather (1)________________ existence. Although they got along fairly well, they did have differences.

List #3 continued

Yolanda had lived a long happy life and began to think that she was 2)_____________. She thought that she would never get hurt or die, no matter what she did. Also, her parents had always told her, "For a gnome, you are quite pretty." Therefore, all her life, Yolanda had been extremely (3)_______________. She just loved looking in the mirror at her tall, slender self.

Miranda was more realistic. She knew she was both (4)_______________ and ugly. She could also be (5) _______________ at times, imagining the worst would happen. In fact, she was sure that she would meet a (6)_______________end if she ever left the house.

Another reason Miranda didn't leave the house was that she was ashamed of her ugly appearance. When she had to look in the mirror to cut her long scraggly hair, she (7)_______________ from the sight and (8)_______________ in the corner for hours afterward. At times like this, her roommate Yolanda, felt (9)_____________ for her and would venture into the forest to dig up some ginger root, Miranda's favorite treat.

One day when Miranda was feeling especially down, Yolanda went out to look for ginger root. However, this time she didn't come back. Miranda waited patiently for a whole year, getting more and more depressed. Finally, she ventured outside to find her roommate.

As she walked deep into the forest, she heard Yolanda's voice. Soon she came upon Yolanda sitting on a tree stump with a handsome, smiling troll.

"Where have you been? Why didn't you ever come back?" Miranda asked angrily.

"Well, the last time I went out looking for ginger root to cheer you up, I met Sebastian," said Yolanda. "He was so (10)_______________ and happy about life that I realized I couldn't go back home and face your gloom anymore. I'm sorry if I caused you any worry."

Miranda frowned at the happy couple. "I suppose your leaving has nothing at all to do with his good looks," she commented.

Yolanda just smiled.

Super Challenge

Directions: Use the bonus words from the list on the test to finish the story above.

Vocabulary List #4

fluent: able to write or speak easily and smoothly

- Roberto is bilingual; he is **fluent** in both Spanish and English.
- The ambassador was looking for an interpreter who was **fluent** in Portuguese.

console: to comfort; to make someone feel less sad

- Brenda's friends **consoled** her when her dog died.
- He **consoled** himself with a hot fudge sundae after he failed his English test.

memorabilia: things worth remembering

- Mrs. Jenkins' closet is filled with hula hoops, poodle skirts and other **memorabilia** from the 1950s.
- Mr. Lindstrom had lots of World War II **memorabilia**, including some medals, a number of photos and his discharge papers.

expectorate: to spit

- The dentist asked Molly to **expectorate** into the sink.
- Bart climbed off his horse, brushed off his jeans and **expectorated** on the dirt street. The sheriff told him to get back on his horse and get out of town.

egotistical: conceited; selfish

- "If you constantly brag, people may start thinking you are **egotistical**," Jean warned her sister. "They probably won't like you, either."
- Although the straight *A* student was really modest about his accomplishments, everyone thought he was **egotistical** because of the way his mother carried on and on about him. Actually, his mother was the **egotistical** one.

meager: small in amount

- "Halloween hand-outs were **meager** this year," said Chris. "I only got three pieces of taffy and a Skittle."
- Theo scowled when he saw the **meager** portion of food on his plate. Was his mother putting him on a diet?

maternal: motherly; having to do with mothers

- "Our old cat surprised us by behaving in such a **maternal** way toward the new kitten my dad brought home," said Melissa.
- Danielle was always very **maternal,** so it was no surprise when she and her husband decided to have a child.

guffaw: a loud, coarse burst of laughter

- Carl told jokes because he loved to hear **guffaws** from the guys.
- The comedian wasn't satisfied with just chuckles. He wanted **guffaws** from the audience.

amble: to walk slowly or leisurely

- Nick **ambled** in 40 minutes late, ignoring the stares of everyone in the crowd.
- Susan **ambled** along the street, admiring the window displays.

monotonous: boring because it's all the same

- "Having to write your spelling words 50 times each would be a **monotonous** task," Mr. Donaldson said.
- Mr. Boris threw his son's toy drum in the garbage can. He couldn't stand the **monotonous** beat any longer.

Bonus Words

★avaricious: greedy

- The **avaricious** storekeeper cheated little kids by giving them the wrong change for the candy they bought.
- For the **avaricious** billionaire, no amount of money was ever enough.

★gumption: initiative and courage; "get-up-and-go"

- "I'm sorry you didn't make the basketball team, but I am proud of you anyway," said LeRoy's father. "It took a lot of **gumption** for someone as short as you to try out."
- It took a lot of **gumption** for Sally to start her own company.

Name ______________________________

Test

Matching

Match each word in the left column to its correct definition in the right column.

____ 1. memorabilia
____ 2. expectorate
____ 3. monotonous
____ 4. egotistical
____ 5. amble
____ 6. console
____ 7. meager
____ 8. maternal
____ 9. fluent
____ 10. guffaw

★Bonus Words
____ 11. gumption
____ 12. avaricious

a. able to write or speak easily and smoothly
b. a loud, coarse burst of laughter
c. to comfort; to make someone feel less sad
d. greedy
e. a sound made by elephants when they are angry
f. boring because it's all the same
g. things worth remembering
h. to spit
i. to walk slowly or leisurely
j. a blue liquid used for cleaning
k. small in amount
l. motherly; having to do with mothers
m. cousinly; having to do with cousins
n. conceited; selfish
o. initiative and courage; "get-up-and-go"

Fill-in-the-Blank

Directions: The first 10 words listed above belong in the story below. Read the story and use the clues in the text to place each word in the correct blank space provided. You may change the form of a word to fit the story, if you need to. (For example, you might need to add *ed, ing, ly* or *s*.)

Unforgettable

Antonio's English assignment was to write about an "unforgettable character" in his life, and he was having a hard time with it. If the assignment had been to write about a "beautiful character," it would have been easy. Tracy, who sat next to him in math class, would have been the perfect subject. A "(1)________________character" would have been easy, too — his mother.

A "just plain disgusting" character would have been his brother Hank, who belched the alphabet backwards every morning at breakfast and finished his show by threatening to (2)________________ in Antonio's cereal if he didn't applaud.

"Unforgettable character," though, was hard. Hank was unforgettable, but not in a good way. Besides, he didn't want to think about Hank any more than he had to.

Finally Antonio's mother suggested that he visit Uncle Lou, his father's oldest brother. Antonio liked that idea. He had always enjoyed Uncle Lou.

Antonio hadn't seen Uncle Lou since his grandmother's funeral three months ago. Uncle Lou was so sad that day that Antonio couldn't talk to him without getting tears in his eyes. No one, not even Antonio's father, could (3)________________ him. He just hung his head and hardly said a word. Whenever he did speak, it was in Spanish, and Antonio had a hard time understanding him. Uncle Lou was the only one left in the family who was (4)________________ in Spanish.

As Antonio (5)________________ down Uncle Lou's street, he spotted a familiar figure walking just as slowly toward him.

"Hey, little Antonio, how are you?" yelled Uncle Lou, and he let out a loud (6)________________. Antonio had always loved Uncle Lou's weird laugh. He also loved the way he played the accordion at family weddings and soon had everyone dancing, even people who said they didn't dance.

When they entered Uncle Lou's new apartment, Antonio was surprised at the (7)________________ furnishings. They each took a chair (the only two pieces of furniture in the living room), and Antonio noticed that the walls were covered with interesting baseball (8)________________. There were gloves, caps, a broken bat and pictures of Lou in a baseball uniform.

"What's all this?" Antonio asked. He didn't know Lou had ever played baseball.

"I played ball for the Chicago Cubs 30 years ago. I don't want to be (9)________________ and brag, but I batted .300," smiled Uncle Lou.

List #4 continued

For the next three hours, Uncle Lou told stories about his short but exciting baseball career. Antonio enjoyed the stories and didn't even find it (10)________________ when Uncle Lou repeated some of them several times. Antonio knew that he would have a lot to write about for his English assignment.

He also couldn't wait to impress Tracy with the fact that his very own uncle had played for the Chicago Cubs.

Later, he remembered that he hadn't asked about Uncle Lou's furniture. What had happened to it? Maybe there was another story there . . .

Super Challenge

Directions: Use the bonus words from the list on the test to finish the story above.

____

____

____

____

____

____

____

____

____

____

____

____

	1	2	3	4	5	6	7	8
V	omen	console	intoxicated	dictator	mortal	hoodwink	expectorate	bicker
O	pessimistic	annual	picayune ★	sulk	grotesque	compassion	fragile	glutton
C	immortal	swagger	feline	monotonous	palatial	jacktar ★	tyrant	egotistical
A	irate	optimistic	burnoose ★	gawk	flibbertigibbet ★	vain	barbaric	dumbfounded
B	memorabilia	brutal	gargantuan	vast	guffaw	toxic	prompt	fluent
R	gumption	vivid	mugwump ★	soothe	recoil	blunder	avaricious	inveigle ★
A	obese	maternal	tragic	waiver	hegira ★	amble	ghee ★	meager

Vocabulary List #5

intricate: complicated; involved; detailed

- Mrs. Moskowitz crocheted **intricate** patterns into her beautiful afghans.
- The plot of *Miss Polly Got a Dolly* was so **intricate** that Tina was confused after the first chapter.

dank: unpleasantly damp

- The basement of the abandoned mansion was **dank** and dark and full of creepy, crawly creatures.
- Frogs need a **dank** environment in order to survive.

lackluster: dull; lacking brightness

- The golden retriever's coat was usually so shiny, but it looked **lackluster** after the dog rolled in the dirt for 10 minutes.
- Carrie fired Troy's band because the group's performances were becoming rather **lackluster**.

inaudible: unable to be heard

- The noise coming from the closet was nearly **inaudible**, but Jeremy thought he heard the sound of a whimpering puppy.
- The sound was so soft it was almost **inaudible**. Still, at 3:00 AM, it scared Rick half to death.

dismember: to cut or tear off the limbs

- Rachel was pretty sure she could sit through the horror movie. However, when the zombies started to **dismember** a giraffe, she had to leave.
- While her family tried to finish dinner, Stacy explained how her biology class **dismembered** a frog.

submerge: to place under water

- The swimming teacher won't let us leave class until we have completely **submerged** our heads in the pool.
- Billy **submerged** his rubber ducky in the bath tub.

lustrous: shiny; glossy

- From the top of the mountain, Harold admired the **lustrous** light reflected off the ski slopes.
- The movie star's **lustrous** hair shimmered under the huge stage lights.

inebriated: drunk

- The **inebriated** man was lucky he wasn't killed when he drove his car into the side of a cement truck.
- Johnny never believed the wild stories his neighbor told when she was **inebriated**.

ponder: to think deeply or consider carefully

- The old man loved to sit on a park bench all day and **ponder** the meaning of life.
- Camille's mother sent her to her room to **ponder** why hitting her little sister was wrong.

authentic: genuine; real

- The man was arrested because the signature on his check was not **authentic**.
- "This is an **authentic** 1920s hairbrush," explained the antique dealer. "That's why I'm charging $60 for it."

Bonus Words

★**compel:** to force

- Because the evidence was so overwhelming, the jury felt **compelled** to find Sam guilty.
- Because Lorraine was so nasty to the customers, her supervisor at Pizza Palace was **compelled** to fire her.

★**genial:** cheerful; friendly

- Katie is always smiling. She is the most **genial** person at school.
- Conrad is not particularly funny or brilliant, but everybody likes him because he is so **genial**.

Name ______________________________

Test

Matching

Match each word in the left column to its correct definition in the right column.

____ 1. intricate
____ 2. dank
____ 3. ponder
____ 4. lackluster
____ 5. inaudible
____ 6. dismember
____ 7. submerge
____ 8. authentic
____ 9. lustrous
____ 10. inebriated

★Bonus Words
____ 11. genial
____ 12. compel

a. dull; lacking brightness
b. another name for anchovy pizza
c. unable to be heard
d. complicated; involved; detailed
e. to force
f. to cut or tear off the limbs
g. tattoo design
h. cheerful; friendly
i. to place under water
j. unpleasantly damp
k. shiny; glossy
l. drunk
m. an important ingredient in shampoo
n. to think deeply or consider carefully
o. genuine; real

Fill-in-the-Blank

Directions: The first 10 words listed above belong in the story below. Read the story and use the clues in the text to place each word in the correct blank space provided. You may change the form of a word to fit the story, if you need to. (For example, you might need to add *ed, ing, ly* or *s*.)

Treasure Hunt

It was midnight and everyone was asleep except Carmine and Felix. They stood on a dock looking out into a dark bay where an old ship was partially (1)________________. Only its top half stuck out of the water. The ship had sailed the seas in the 1600s, and time had (2)__________________ it, pulling its shutters from its hinges, loosening the planking and forming holes in its belly.

According to the treasure map Carmine and Felix had found a few days earlier, a large treasure chest was hidden on the ship. The boys were determined to find it.

Neither of the boys owned a boat, so they had to spend a lot of time (3)_______________ the problem of how to get out to the ship. They thought long and hard. Finally, Carmine came up with a solution.

"I know an old sailor who gives boat rides when he's not (4)_____________. When he's drunk, he can't steer straight and it's dangerous to ride with him, but maybe he will be available to take us out to the ship."

As it turned out, Hank, the sailor, was sober that night. Carmine and Felix climbed aboard.

The full moon was so (5)________________ that it lit their way. Its brightness also made it possible for them to see the map clearly. "That map looks very (6)________________ and hard to understand. Can you really find treasure with such a complicated map?" Hank asked, with a mischievous look on his face.

"We're going to try," said Felix.

Hank's little boat pulled up next to the ship. Carmine and Felix jumped into the water, swam onto the ship deck and headed down the stairs to the hold.

The inside of the ship smelled (7)________________ and musty. They walked around cautiously, fearing that the floor might cave in under their feet. They studied the map and followed the directions to the treasure trunk.

It was just where the map said it would be. As the boys fell to their knees in front of the trunk, they heard an almost (8)_______________ moan. Because the sound was so faint, they ignored it. They pried the trunk lid open and stared with disappointment at thousands of (9)________________ coins.

"I thought gold was supposed to be shiny," Felix said. "I don't think these coins are (10)_________________. They look fake. Let's just take a couple home to look at."

Suddenly the moaning grew louder. The boys turned and jumped to their feet. Two red eyes glowed from a shadowed corner.

"I'm out of here!" screamed Carmine. The boys dove into the water without any coins and swam away from the ship.

Nearly out of breath, they pulled themselves onto Hank's boat and begged him to high-tail it to shore. "So, you boys saw something in that ship, did you?" said Hank with a smile.

Super Challenge

Directions: Use the bonus words from the list on the test to finish the story above.

Vocabulary List #6

jovial: jolly

- Martha's grandfather was the only **jovial** relative she had. All the others were always whining about something.
- Isaiah's **jovial** laugh is contagious.

careen: to tip or swerve from side to side

- They heard the squeal of brakes as the car **careened** around the corner.
- Tracy lost control of her skateboard and **careened** into the chain link fence.

minuscule: very small

- Most insects are **minuscule**, but some roaches can grow as long as an adult's thumb.
- Even though the pimple on Mitzi's nose was **minuscule**, she thought it was the size of Mt. Everest.

squalor: miserable, filthy conditions

- Whenever we visit my sister's apartment, my dad gets upset about the **squalor** she lives in.
- The family had to live in **squalor** for two years before they could afford to rent a decent place.

morbid: gruesome

- Shannon thought the ax in Del's head was way too **morbid**, even if it was fake.
- Carolyn thought her grandparents were getting entirely too **morbid**. All they talked about were their illnesses and their funeral plans.

wrath: anger; fury

- Janice avoided her father's **wrath** by staying in her room until his good humor returned.
- Laura experienced her parents' **wrath** when she had a party without their permission while they were out of town.

grimace: a facial contortion expressing pain or disgust

- Perry's mom could tell when he **grimaced** that there was no way he was going to eat the broccoli yogurt she had placed in front of him.
- Lauren **grimaced** when she saw her report card. "I think I would rather not go home tonight," she said.

pseudonym: false name; pen name

- "Dr. Seuss" is the **pseudonym** for Theodor Geisel.
- Some people use **pseudonyms** because they don't want their real name to be known.

tranquil: peaceful; calm

- When Marilyn comes home from work, she turns on **tranquil** music and lies down on the couch for half an hour.
- "I saw grazing deer in the quiet meadow," said Tiffany. "It was a **tranquil** scene."

sallow: yellowish and pale

- Angel hated her dull brown hair and **sallow** complexion. She longed for raven hair and rosy cheeks.
- After having the stomach flu for five days, Yogi looked **sallow**.

Bonus Words

★intermittent: not continuous; stopping and starting

- The weather forecaster said there would be **intermittent** showers on Saturday.
- Although Kevin tried to eat nutritious meals, he did have **intermittent** cravings for greasy chili cheese fries.

★a cappella: without musical instruments as accompaniment

- The choir's piano player got to rest during the song that the group sang **a cappella**.
- When all the orchestra instruments were stolen, the chorus had to perform their concert **a cappella**.

Name ______________________________

Test

Matching

Match each word in the left column to its correct definition in the right column.

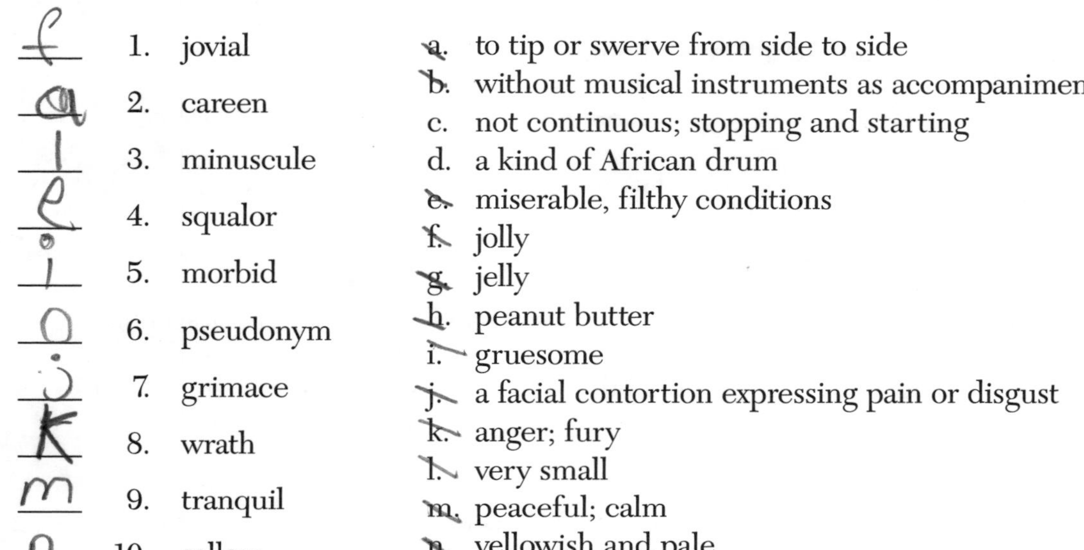

____ 1. jovial	a. to tip or swerve from side to side
____ 2. careen	b. without musical instruments as accompaniment
____ 3. minuscule	c. not continuous; stopping and starting
____ 4. squalor	d. a kind of African drum
____ 5. morbid	e. miserable, filthy conditions
____ 6. pseudonym	f. jolly
____ 7. grimace	g. jelly
____ 8. wrath	h. peanut butter
____ 9. tranquil	i. gruesome
____ 10. sallow	j. a facial contortion expressing pain or disgust
	k. anger; fury
	l. very small
	m. peaceful; calm
	n. yellowish and pale
	o. false name; pen name

★Bonus Words

____ 11. intermittent

____ 12. a cappella

Fill-in-the-Blank

Directions: The first 10 words listed above belong in the story below. Read the story and use the clues in the text to place each word in the correct blank space provided. You may change the form of a word to fit the story, if you need to. (For example, you might need to add *ed, ing, ly* or *s*.)

Grandpa Sam's Story of the Raisin

My Grandpa Sam and I love to pass away the evenings on the big porch swing in front of our house. We sip lemonade to cool off, and sometimes a gentle breeze blows through as we rock back and forth. It's so (1)______________ outside that I could fall asleep if it weren't for Grandpa's lively stories. He's a (2)______________ man who keeps me laughing. One evening I asked him about "Old Man Ventana," who lives in the rundown house at the end of the street.

"Now there is an interesting story," he began, which is how he always begins stories. "Old Man Ventana" was not always his name; that's just a (3)_______________. His real name is Claude Raisin, and he invented the raisin.

"Even though he was an inventor by trade, his invention of the raisin came by chance. He was a forgetful sort of guy, and one day he came upon a bag of grapes he had left on the windowsill three days before. Instead of the big plump juicy grapes he had left there, he found a bag full of (4)_______________ shriveled up black things. Besides being forgetful, he was a tad adventurous. He popped one of those shriveled little things in his mouth and discovered that it tasted pretty good.

"After that, Claude gave up all his other inventions to concentrate on the dead-looking grapes. He was hoping that they would be his ticket out of the (5)_______________ he was living in. He named the snack after himself because he was just about as wrinkled as the raisin. By the way, he also had that same sickly, (6)_______________ complexion that he has now.

"Anyway, after months of working, Claude decided to introduce the raisins nationwide, just in time for Halloween. He thought that shriveled up dead-looking berries would make a perfect treat for the (7)_______________ holiday. He was thrilled when parents started buying raisins right along with Halloween candy because the raisins were nutritious. But he knew the real test would come on Halloween, when he could watch the kids' reactions. On Halloween night, he hid in the bushes and watched as boys and girls knocked on doors.

"Much to Claude's dismay, all the kids (8) _______________ when they received a box of raisins. Well, besides being forgetful and adventuresome, Claude also had a pretty hot temper. After about the twentieth frown, he jumped out of the bushes, red-faced and full of (9)_______________. The whole neighborhood watched him climb in his old pickup and (10)_______________ down our street at full speed. He never talked to anyone on the street again, and he soon changed his name to Claude Ventana."

"Really?" I asked. "What happened to the raisins?"

"Well, you eat them, don't you?"

"Not when I can help it. I hate raisins."

Grandpa Sam shook his head. "'Old Man Ventana' would not be happy to hear that."

Super Challenge

Directions: Use the bonus words from the test to finish the story above.

____

____

____

____

____

____

____

____

____

____

____

____

Vocabulary List #7

cordial: warm and friendly

- Heidi was **cordial** to Mr. Fugi when he was introduced as the new principal.
- Leonard was nervous about meeting the president, but she greeted him with such a **cordial** handshake that he soon felt very comfortable.

acquitted: found not guilty

- Bud's friends were all relieved when he was **acquitted** of the charges against him.
- Because Gina was **acquitted** of shoplifting, she did not have to go to jail.

virtue: goodness; moral excellence; a good quality or feature

- Beth's parents can't wait for her to discover the **virtue** of keeping her bedroom clean.
- The senator was a man of great **virtue** and was never once involved in a scandal of any kind.

significant: full of meaning; having great impact

- The strange weather patterns are **significant** because they may suggest an overall change in world climates.
- The gold locket that Denise wears is **significant** to her because it once belonged to her grandmother.

dignity: self respect and honor

- Mr. Santini told his four children to behave with **dignity** at their grandfather's funeral.
- "If you behave with **dignity** in this classroom, you will do well and have my respect," said the new chemistry teacher.

melodramatic: overly emotional

- The actors were so **melodramatic** that it was hard to take the play seriously.
- Midge was being **melodramatic** when she accidentally dumped a slice of pizza in her lap and then shouted, "That does it! I'm never eating again for as long as I live!"

eternal: existing always, without beginning or end

- "My love for you is **eternal**," Romeo whispered. "I will never love another."
- Harvey was **eternally** grateful to his father for letting him drive his Corvette to the prom. He never forgot the favor.

paranoid: overly suspicious

- My sister is **paranoid**. She's convinced that someone is spying on her.
- When Brooke saw that her locker door was ajar, she became **paranoid** and thought everyone in school was trying to steal her stuff.

emerge: to rise from; to become visible or known

- The excited crowd held up banners as the football team **emerged** from the locker room and ran onto the field.
- The very Saturday that Melody was supposed to go out with Gabe, a pimple **emerged** on her forehead.

chaos: extreme confusion or disorder

- The earthquake and power outage threw the city into **chaos**. The police, fire department and ambulances couldn't keep up with all the calls.
- The halls were **chaotic** when the students burst out of the classrooms at the last bell on the last day of school.

Bonus Words

★impeccable: faultless; free of error

- Walter's reading of the poem was **impeccable**. He didn't stumble once, and everyone could hear him clearly.
- JoAnn's taste in clothing was **impeccable**. That's why she was voted "Best Dressed."

★grovel: to humble yourself in a degrading way before someone

- "I guess I'm going to forgive Tim for breaking our date," said Julia, "but I'm going to make him **grovel** first."
- No matter how she **groveled**, Ericka could not persuade her sister to loan her the beautiful black sweater.

List #7

Name ________________________________

Test

Matching

Match each word in the left column to its correct definition in the right column.

____ 1. virtue
____ 2. cordial
____ 3. acquitted
____ 4. significant
____ 5. chaos
____ 6. melodramatic
____ 7. emerge
____ 8. eternal
____ 9. dignity
____ 10. paranoid

★Bonus Words
____ 11. impeccable
____ 12. grovel

a. overly emotional
b. overly suspicious
c. goodness; moral excellence; a good quality or feature
d. full of meaning; having great impact
e. self respect and honor
f. existing always, without beginning or end
g. extreme confusion or disorder
h. nasal spray
i. faultless; free from error
j. to rise from; to become visible or known
k. warm and friendly
l. warm and sweaty
m. writing tool used in the Victorian era
n. to humble yourself in a degrading way before someone
o. found not guilty

Fill-in-the-Blank

Directions: The first 10 words listed above belong in the story below. Read the story and use the clues in the text to place each word in the correct blank space provided. You may change the form of a word to fit the story, if you need to. (For example, you might need to add *ed, ing, ly* or *s*.)

The Trial of Little Miss Muffet

Little Miss Muffet's trial had been publicized in all the major newspapers and on every television station in Gooseland, so when the day of the trial finally came, the steps of the courthouse were a scene of complete (1)________________. Men, women, children, dogs, cats with fiddles, even dishes and spoons crowded the courthouse stairs, awaiting Miss

Muffet's arrival. Reporters with notepads, microphones and TV cameras were everywhere, eagerly awaiting the trial of the century.

Finally, a limousine pulled up, and Miss Muffet (2)________________ with her lawyer, a certain Mr. Georgie Porgie, right by her side. Reporters immediately began jockeying for positions near the courthouse doors, eager to ask Miss Muffet their questions.

"Did you do it, Miss Muffet? Did you really do it?"

"Did you really knock Humpty Dumpty off the wall and make him break his hip?"

Miss Muffet calmly ignored all this, peering over her dark sunglasses only once to say something to her lawyer.

Once inside the courtroom, though, Miss Muffet lost her calm poise. The weight of the charges against her finally hit. Going to prison would certainly make a (3)________________ change in her life. There probably weren't very many good shops in the prison mall. She looked hard at the jury and feared they would never give her a fair trial. Their feelings for her did not appear to be (4)________________. She saw complete disgust in the expressions on their faces. "They will find me guilty!" she cried to her lawyer. "They hate me. I can see it in their eyes. Everyone hates me. Even my cat hates me."

Her lawyer sighed. "You are just being (5)______________________, Miss Muffet."

The trial began, and witness after witness was called to the stand. When Miss Muffet herself was finally done being cross-examined, she stopped in front of the jury box, fell to her knees, and cried out, "I am a woman of great (6)____________________. There's no way I could ever commit such a horrible, horrible crime as this. I look to you for mercy and justice. And if I don't receive it, I shall be (7)___________________ unhappy. A smile will never again cross these sad, but nonetheless perfectly glossed, lips."

As Miss Muffet touched her lips for effect, Mr. Porgie rolled his eyes, quite annoyed that his client was always so (8)______________________. Couldn't she just act normal for once?

When she turned to him from her position on the floor, he gave her a look which seemed to say "Get up off the floor. Have some (9)________________ for once."

Miss Muffet pulled herself off the floor and quietly returned to her seat.

In the end, Miss Muffet was (10)________________ of the charges against her, all because of the testimony of a certain eight-legged creature. He swore that at the very moment of Humpty Dumpty's fall, he had seen Miss Muffet sitting on a park bench after her morning jog, eating a high-fiber, low-fat curds and whey breakfast bar.

Super Challenge

Directions: Use the bonus words from the test to finish the story above.

Vocabulary List #8

hostile: very unfriendly

- Lester couldn't understand why people found him so **hostile**. Perhaps it had something to do with the way he scowled and said, "Leave me alone," whenever anyone smiled and said hello to him.
- Mary knew she owed her father an apology for acting so **hostile** when he told her to get off the phone.

anguish: great suffering

- Elizabeth's **anguish** at the death of her cat affected all her friends and relatives.
- Rory knew something was wrong when she saw the expression of **anguish** on her father's face.

boisterous: noisy and rowdy

- Grandma loved the **boisterous** children, but she was used to a quiet life. She had to admit they got on her nerves after only ten minutes.
- The swimming pool sign read, "No **boisterous** play." Donny thought, "I suppose this means I can't chase my brother around the pool edge, push him in and dunk him."

interrogate: to question

- Tyler's favorite part of the police show is when the detectives **interrogate** the crime suspects.
- Every time Dawn left the house, her father **interrogated** her about where she was going, who she was going with and what she was going to do.

bogus: fake; phony; counterfeit

- The **bogus** offer involved a supposedly free trip to Acapulco.
- Henry thought he was going to be making $20.00 an hour, but it turned out that the job offer was **bogus**. He would be making only 75 cents an hour.

charisma: quality in a person that inspires or attracts others; charm or allure

- The candidate had so much **charisma** that huge crowds gathered every time she spoke.
- Mr. Wonka was the most popular teacher at school. His **charisma** made going to class a pleasure.

dilapidated: falling to pieces; broken down

- The **dilapidated** house was said to be haunted by a headless old woman.
- The old junk yard was full of **dilapidated** automobiles and household appliances.

ecstatic: joyous; extremely happy

- James was **ecstatic** when he got Michael Jordon's autograph.
- The children were **ecstatic** when they heard they were flying to Disneyland for their vacation.

sinister: evil

- Louisa knew it wasn't just her imagination. Something **sinister** lurked in the shadows, and she shivered at the thought of what it might be.
- The man in the dark overcoat had a **sinister** look about him, so Pat and Kelly immediately turned around and walked the other direction.

philanthropist: a person (usually wealthy) who gives money to charity

- Andrew Carnegie, the great **philanthropist**, established foundations to give money to worthwhile causes.
- The Montgomery brothers couldn't be any more different from one another. While Bryon was a great **philanthropist**, Milton was stingy with his money.

Bonus Words

★ambiguous: unclear; having more than one meaning

- The math assignment was so **ambiguous** that none of the students knew exactly what they were supposed to do.
- Rita got lost trying to find her new school because the directions she had been given were **ambiguous**.

★befuddle: to confuse

- Mr. Macfee never did his own taxes because the tax forms always **befuddled** him.
- The whole class was **befuddled** by Mrs. Stafford's lecture on adverbial phrases.

Directions: The first 10 words listed above belong in the story below. Read the story and

Name ______________________________

Test

Matching

Match each word in the left column to its correct definition in the right column.

____ 1. ecstatic	a.	very unfriendly
____ 2. philanthropist	b.	falling to pieces; broken down
____ 3. hostile	c.	great suffering
____ 4. boisterous	d.	a person who studies old bones
____ 5. bogus	e.	noisy and rowdy
____ 6. charisma	f.	unclear; having more than one meaning
____ 7. interrogate	g.	to question
____ 8. dilapidated	h.	fake; phony; counterfeit
____ 9. anguish	i.	a person (usually wealthy) who gives money to charity
____ 10. sinister	j.	to confuse
★Bonus Words	k.	quality in a person that inspires or attracts others; charm or allure
____ 11. ambiguous	l.	joyous; extremely happy
____ 12. befuddle	m.	evil
	n.	oval
	o.	Ovaltine

Fill-in-the-Blank

use the clues in the text to place each word in the correct blank space provided. You may change the form of a word to fit the story, if you need to. (For example, you might need to add *ed, ing, ly* or *s*.)

Aliens Invade Day Care

Fran was (1)____________ the day she graduated from journalism school. She was ready to change the world with her wonderful writing and her nose for news. But jobs were harder to come by than she had realized, and after four months of living in a (2)____________ old building in a studio apartment with cockroaches for roommates, she accepted a job with the *Intruder*, the worst tabloid newspaper she had ever seen.

List #8 continued

The newspaper's editor was a (3)______________ man named Mr. Pendragon, who loved embarrassing people and digging up dirt about their lives. Sometimes, when he couldn't find dirt, he made it up. He caused people a lot of (4) ______________ and never even felt guilty. Fran couldn't believe the first assignment he gave her: to investigate reports of alien children at Darla's Day Care.

Darla's Day Care had been started by a (5) ________________ who let needy children attend for free. "You can see why aliens from outer space attend," snorted Mr. Pendragon. "They probably don't have the money to go anywhere else."

Reluctantly, Fran drove to the day care center. The old house on Daffodil Drive was the color of yellow Post-It notes and had a large play area in the back. As Fran walked up to the door, Darla herself came out with a smile to greet her. But when she spotted the *Intruder* badge on Fran's shirt, Darla's smile turned into a frown. She became very (6)______________.

"I'll bet you're here about those 'alien kids' aren't you?" said Darla. "How pathetic. Why don't you get a decent job?"

"I would just like to ask you some questions," said Fran. "I'm really not here to cause trouble."

Darla sighed. "Well, I'll give you the scoop, but I'm not going to let you come in here and (7) _______________ these kids about a space craft or anything. I'll tell you myself how those stories got started. Mrs. Gruman, who lives next door (you can probably see her peeking from behind her curtains), hates kids and has been nasty to me ever since this business opened. First she called the police and said I wasn't properly disciplining these kids. 'Those children are way too (8)______________,' she complained to the police, 'always running around shouting and jumping and laughing.'

"The police took one look and said, 'Lady, they are kids! They are supposed to be active.'

"When the police didn't shut us down, Mrs. Gruman started telling (9)___________ stories about alien children to anyone who would listen. She told wild tales about little green people and a space ship landing at midnight."

Just then seven children came squealing up to Darla.

"Darla! Darla!" they cried. "Is it time to make chocolate chip cookies?"

"Well, Munchkins, it's up to this lady here." She looked at Fran with a winning smile. "Want to help?"

Fran found herself saying, "Yes." The lady certainly had (10) ______________, she thought. She wanted to do whatever Darla wanted her to do. Without even thinking about it, Fran dumped her *Intruder* badge into a wastebasket.

She didn't notice the little green child who fished the badge out of the wastebasket and took it into the space ship parked in the back yard. "Maybe we can use this some day," Gazbot thought as she added the badge to the rest of the things she had taken out of the trash.

Super Challenge

Directions: Use the bonus words from the test to finish the story above.

____

____

____

____

____

____

____

____

____

	1	2	3	4	5	6	7	8
V	lustrous	acquitted	pseudonym	grovel	a cappella	bogus	compel	dilapidated
O	tranquil	melodramatic	zebu ★	philanthropist	lackluster	intermittent	hostile	wrath
C	squalor	intricate	hawser ★	jovial	vichyssoise ★	significant	inebriated	cordial
A	virtue	ylangylang ★	dank	careen	impeccable	peplum ★	authentic	paranoid
B	befuddle	minuscule	emerge	dignity	dismembered	sallow	lederhosen ★	ecstatic
R	submerge	anguish	sinister	genial	charisma	eternal	ambiguous	grimace
A	interrogate	morbid	inaudible	boisterous	gewgaw ★	ponder	katydid ★	chaos

Vocabulary List #9

infatuated: extremely attracted to something or someone

- Brad was hopelessly **infatuated** with Katie, the only girl in his day care group.
- Maria had been **infatuated** with the idea of becoming a Chicago Bear ever since she could remember.

habitually: repeatedly or continuously

- Reality was just not exciting enough for Ralph, so he lied **habitually** whenever he was asked "What's new with you?"
- Since Marty was **habitually** late to class, Ms. Wilson automatically marked him tardy when she took role.

ebony: black; a type of dark, heavy wood

- The black keys on the piano were made out of **ebony**.
- Gina loved Grandpa Romano's dignified look — his snow white beard, his unchanged **ebony** hair and his stately walk.

mortified: humiliated; embarrassed

- Josh was **mortified** when he slipped and fell as he walked on stage to get his diploma.
- Melinda had only one line in the whole play. She was **mortified** when she came on stage and forgot it.

plagiarize: to pass off someone else's words or ideas as your own; to copy

- "If your essay sounds like it came straight from the encyclopedia, I'm going to think you **plagiarized** it," said Mr. Guiterrez.
- The reporter was not just dishonest; he was stupid. He **plagiarized** an article his own boss had written!

venomous: filled with deep hatred

- Vivian shot Liz a **venomous** glare when she saw her talking to her boyfriend.
- Mr. Brown's comments are so **venomous** that no one voluntarily signs up for any of his classes.

List #9 continued

remorseful: filled with sorrow or guilt

- "If you seemed even a little **remorseful** about skipping class, I would go easy on you," said the principal, "but you don't, so I'm assigning you three weeks of detention."
- The last piece of apple pie tasted so good that Dillon wasn't even **remorseful** about eating it — at least not until he saw his mom standing in the doorway watching him.

opaque: not transparent; can't be seen through

- "Move out of the way," Alan yelled at his sister as she stood right in front of the television. "You do know you're **opaque**, don't you?"
- Superman uses X-ray vision to see through **opaque** walls.

guerrilla: having to do with "underground" army members specializing in harassment and sabotage

- The rebel army troops used **guerrilla** tactics to take over the capital city.
- He was killed by **guerrilla** gunfire just before his troops reached the battlefield.

succinct: brief and to the point

- Surprisingly, a **succinct** one-page essay is harder to write than a three-page paper.
- "I'll be **succinct**," said Sophie's mother. "No."

Bonus Words

★vindictive: wanting revenge; unforgiving

- When Paul started a rumor about Kayla just because she broke off their date, she knew he was being **vindictive**.
- "I know the reason I didn't get invited to Kelly's party is because of that remark I made," said Joella. "She can be so **vindictive**."

★amend: to change for the better; to remove faults

- The citizens of Elkville decided to **amend** the constitution to allow gambling.
- The Harley Club decided that the minutes should be **amended** to include the results of the vote taken at the last meeting.

Name ______________________________

Test

Matching

Match each word in the left column to its correct definition in the right column.

____ 1. infatuated
____ 2. habitually
____ 3. ebony
____ 4. mortified
____ 5. succinct
____ 6. plagiarize
____ 7. remorseful
____ 8. guerrilla
____ 9. venomous
____ 10. opaque

★Bonus Words

____ 11. vindictive
____ 12. amend

a. extremely attracted to something or someone
b. filled with sorrow or guilt
c. a very large member of the ape family
d. brief and to the point
e. filled with deep hatred
f. filled with chocolate and pecans and whipped cream
g. humiliated; embarrassed
h. not transparent; can't be seen through
i. black; a type of dark, heavy wood
j. to pass off someone else's words or ideas as your own; to copy
k. kind of ventilation used in subway systems
l. to change for the better; to remove faults
m. wanting revenge; unforgiving
n. repeatedly or continuously
o. having to do with "underground" army members specializing in harassment and sabotage

Fill-in-the-Blank

Directions: The first 10 words listed above belong in the story below. Read the story and use the clues in the text to place each word in the correct blank space provided. You may change the form of a word to fit the story, if you need to. (For example, you might need to add *ed, ing, ly* or *s.*)

Daydreams

Elvis became (1)________________ with Lydia back in September, right when school started. She was all he could think about. He stared at the back of her head in math class every day. Her long (2)______________ hair reminded him of black licorice, his favorite candy. He imagined that the country had been taken over by terrorists and that he had to protect Lydia from bombings and other (3)________________ actions. She would be so grateful for his bravery that she would run into his arms.

Lydia replaced English as Elvis' favorite subject. He used to love reading stories, writing reports, and taking spelling tests. But now all he did was stare at the wall behind Ms. Goldberg, wishing with his whole heart that the wall wasn't (4)________________. Then he could see through it into Lydia's science class next door. Alas, it was not to be.

"Elvis. Elvis Stratton, I want to talk to you, Mister," demanded a voice. Elvis recognized the anger in Ms. Goldberg's voice. He had heard it a lot lately, and it was always directed at him.

"You are (5)________________ daydreaming in my class, and it has gone on far too long. Every day you come in here and just stare at the wall. If you don't change your ways, Mister, we're going to have some problems."

Elvis turned bright red. He was (6)________________ to be yelled at in front of the whole class. And he hated it when she called him "Mister."

"And that's not the only bone I have to pick with you, Mister. The report on William Shakespeare that you turned in last week sounds way too much like the encyclopedia. Did you (7)________________ it?"

Elvis was immediately (8)________________. He knew he shouldn't have copied the encyclopedia, but he had spent all his time writing poems for Lydia. By the time he remembered he had a report, it was due the next day. Right then he decided he would never put off his school work again. He would put Lydia out of his mind forever and always do his homework a week ahead of time. But even though he was sorry for what he had done, he didn't think Ms. Goldberg needed to be so harsh with him.

He hoped Lydia never talked to him that way when they were married. He could see it now. They would get married in a little church in a meadow. Her current boyfriend, Paul, would be very angry that she was marrying Elvis. Because he would undoubtedly have

(9) _______________ feelings for Elvis, Paul would try to ruin the wedding. (People who are filled with hatred sometimes do that sort of thing.) When the minister said, "Does anyone know why these two should not be joined in marriage?" Paul would stand up and shout, "I do! Elvis is a criminal! He plagiarized a report in 8th grade!"

"It doesn't matter!" Lydia would shout. "I love him!" Those three little words would fill Elvis with joy. Her (10)_______________ statement would lead, he was sure, to a lifetime of happiness.

Elvis smiled.

"And what's so funny about that, Mister?" Elvis looked up at Mrs. Goldberg. For a moment, he was puzzled. What was she doing at his wedding?

Super Challenge

Directions: Use the bonus words from the test to finish the story above.

____

____

____

____

____

____

____

____

____

____

____

Vocabulary List #10

taboo: strongly forbidden

- Since she has already broken one dish, it is now **taboo** for Angela to touch her mom's china.
- Talking about weird Aunt Lorraine was **taboo** at Rick's house, at least around company.

persnickety: too fussy or picky

- Mark is so **persnickety** about his hair that he is always combing it or looking at it in the mirror.
- Cheri's grandma is so **persnickety** about manners she won't speak to anyone who hasn't sent her a thank-you card within one week of receiving a gift.

haphazard: random; by accident; not planned

- The **haphazard** placement of the spice jars made it difficult for Chang to find the spice he wanted when he wanted it.
- Since Eric and Shay's bikes were lying **haphazardly** in the driveway, their dad had to park the car on the street.

imperceptible: very slight; hardly noticeable

- Mario's little brother cried and carried on, even though the bump on his head was almost **imperceptible**.
- The difference in color between the two paint samples was **imperceptible**.

atheist: someone who doesn't believe there is a god

- Salina doesn't pray or go to church because she is an **atheist**.
- A group of **atheists** protested the use of a Nativity scene at the courthouse.

shun: to intentionally avoid someone

- Regina's friends were **shunning** her, so she tried to make the best out of eating lunch and walking to class alone.
- Since Patsy wouldn't let Kurt borrow her new camera, all his friends **shunned** her.

anecdote: a short entertaining story

- The biography of Abraham Lincoln was full of interesting **anecdotes** about his life.
- Uncle Bill is full of **anecdotes** about his years as a stunt man. He said that he once had to jump from a moving car that was on fire.

concur: to agree; to have the same opinion

- As depressing as it was, Brandy had to **concur** with Melissa's observation that the only cute boy in the whole town was Robert, who already had a girl-friend.
- His mother and his teacher **concurred** that Travis had a problem, but they could not agree on how to solve it.

vivacious: full of life; spirited

- Annie was so friendly and **vivacious** that people always enjoyed being around her.
- Keenan was such a **vivacious** child that he had an extra hard time sitting still and keeping quiet in church.

perplexed: confused, puzzled or bewildered

- Gretchen was **perplexed** by her brother's odd behavior. She couldn't figure out why he was suddenly taking showers all the time and wearing after shave lotion.
- The mayor wasn't very smart. Even the simplest problems **perplexed** him.

Bonus Words

★ **capitulate:** to give up; to stop resisting

- After her sons whined and promised to help with the dishes every night for the rest of their lives, Ms. Zeller **capitulated** and let them go to the concert.
- The father finally **capitulated** to the kidnapper's demands and paid the ransom.

★ **consensus:** general agreement

- The **consensus** in the classroom was that there should be no more home-work.
- There was seldom a **consensus** in the Hegge household, but tonight, every-one agreed that ordering a pizza would be a good idea.

Name ________________________________

Test

Matching

Match each word in the left column to its correct definition in the right column.

____ 1. shun
____ 2. persnickety
____ 3. taboo
____ 4. perplexed
____ 5. haphazard
____ 6. imperceptible
____ 7. vivacious
____ 8. atheist
____ 9. concur
____ 10. anecdote

★ **Bonus Words**

____ 11. capitulate
____ 12. consensus

a. general agreement
b. very slight; hardly noticeable
c. a road sign warning of danger
d. someone who doesn't believe there is a god
e. to intentionally avoid someone
f. to agree; to have the same opinion
g. confused, puzzled or bewildered
h. a short entertaining story
i. a long, boring story about "when I was your age," usually told by a parent
j. random; by accident; not planned
k. full of life; spirited
l. too fussy or picky
m. strongly forbidden
n. required by law
o. to give up; to stop resisting

Fill-in-the-Blank

Directions: The first 10 words listed above belong in the story below. Read the story and use the clues in the text to place each word in the correct blank space provided. You may change the form of a word to fit the story, if you need to. (For example, you might need to add *ed, ing, ly* or *s*.)

A Caveman's Tale

Og sat on a rock in his cave, bored with his prehistoric life and the turn it had taken. Og's wife was forever redecorating the cave. She had just changed from a dinosaur theme to a softer more relaxing glacier look for the winter. Og was (1)____________________ by how (2)____________________ Uba was about her decorating. He couldn't figure her out. She would re-draw a picture on the cave's wall five or six times (probably more, really, but Og couldn't count any higher than that), just so it would be perfectly straight. Then she would ask Og which drawing looked straighter, the one that was up now or the one that she had just erased. Since the difference between the two was (3)________________ to Og, he tried to figure out what his wife's opinion was. Then he always (4)________________. If it had been up to Og, he would have drawn the pictures on the walls in a (5)________________ fashion, scribbling one here and one there and not worrying about whether or not anything was straight.

As Og watched his wife carefully arrange a group of multi-sized pebbles at the cave's opening, to create a welcoming entrance for visitors, he thought back to his younger days. He had been a young man with a (6)________________ spirit and enough energy to conquer the world (which, admittedly, was not that large, since only 20 square miles of it had been discovered so far). He had been a lively lad with less of a stoop to his posture than his Neanderthal cousins.

Now, though, he was a bent over old man whose stories nobody wanted to hear. He used to enjoy sitting with the boys exchanging (7)________________. He would tell about the time he pulled a saber-toothed tiger's tail, and that would remind his best friend Ak of the time he found a woolly mammoth hair in his soup. Yes, he and Ak had had some real adventures together.

Og missed Ak. As of two months ago, Ak was being (8)________________ by the clan for being an (9)________________. He had stood up at a clan meeting one day and said he just plain didn't believe in any kind of god anymore. The shocked people responded by kicking him out of the village for three months. There was still one full month before Ak could return, and Og wasn't sure he could bear it. Since it was (10)________________ for

Og to go out and see poor Ak, he missed his friend terribly. He would have counted the days until his return, if only he had been able to count that high.

"What do you think about these wooly mammoth tusks on the wall?" Uba said, interrupting his train of thought.

"Who cares?" thought Og to himself. To Uba, he said, "They look nice, dear."

He sighed. When would life get more interesting? How long would it be before television was invented?

Super Challenge

Directions: Use the bonus words from the test to finish the story above.

Vocabulary List #11

infinite: never-ending; going on forever

- Her mother seemed to have an **infinite** number of questions about Jenny's date with Silas.
- The teacher had **infinite** patience and never lost her temper, no matter how far her students pushed her.

abduct: to kidnap

- Mrs. Jenkin's biggest fear was that her daughter would be **abducted**, so she watched her closely whenever they went to the park.
- Kent's parents didn't believe his story about being **abducted** by aliens and taken away in their spaceship for three hours.

textiles: woven materials; cloth

- The interior designer had a collection of **textiles** for her customers to browse through.
- Clothing manufacturers make many purchases from **textile** factories.

loathe: to hate

- George **loathed** cooked carrots and groaned every time his dad made them for dinner.
- "I **loathe** cleaning the toilet," said Mike. "I'd rather vacuum the whole house every day for a week."

unscrupulous: dishonest; immoral

- The **unscrupulous** coach encouraged his team to cheat whenever they could.
- The businessman was so **unscrupulous** that he cheated people who lived in nursing homes.

controversial: debatable; likely to cause disagreement

- The decision to eliminate school uniforms at St. Mary's School was quite **controversial**.
- Many of Madonna's music videos are **controversial**.

List #11 continued

turbulent: wild; unstable

- Everyone wishes Molly and Zeke would break up. They have such a **turbulent** relationship.
- The injured seal was having trouble staying afloat in the **turbulent** waters.

nocturnal: active at night

- Many owls are **nocturnal**. That's why they see so well in the dark.
- "My cat is **nocturnal** and loves to go out at 2:00 AM," said Marta.

tout: to praise highly

- James Brown has been **touted** as the "Godfather of Soul."
- Mr. Octave had been **touted** as one of the best drama directors in the state, so the school was delighted to hire him.

smug: self-satisfied to an annoying degree

- Marcos was **smug** about the *A* he got on his grammar test. He bragged about it to anyone who would listen.
- Charla was **smug** about knowing the answer when no one else did.

Bonus Words

★ façade: the face or front part of something, especially an artificial or false front

- Jessica's bravery was just a **facade**. Deep down, she was terrified.
- The building had a brick **facade**, but it was really constructed of wood.

★ vehement: forceful; full of intense feeling

- Ella took a **vehement** dislike to tomatoes after she ate too many of them and got sick.
- The defendant **vehemently** denied having stolen the car.

Name ______________________________

Test

Matching

Match each word in the left column to its correct definition in the right column.

____ 1. infinite
____ 2. controversial
____ 3. textiles
____ 4. nocturnal
____ 5. tout
____ 6. smug
____ 7. unscrupulous
____ 8. turbulent
____ 9. loathe
____ 10. abduct

★ **Bonus Words**

____ 11. vehement
____ 12. façade

a. to kidnap
b. the face or front part of something, especially an artificial or false front
c. woven materials; cloth
d. wild; unstable
e. a small bag used to carry lemons
f. to hate
g. to praise highly
h. self-satisfied to an annoying degree
i. dishonest; immoral
j. a nutritious vegetable that most kids hate
k. spinach
l. debatable; likely to cause disagreement
m. never-ending; going on forever
n. active at night
o. forceful; full of intense feeling

Fill-in-the-Blank

Directions: The first 10 words listed above belong in the story below. Read the story and use the clues in the text to place each word in the correct blank space provided. You may change the form of a word to fit the story, if you need to. (For example, you might need to add *ed, ing, ly* or *s*.)

Sooper Dooper Grocery Guy

Gus, also known as the "Sooper Dooper Grocery Guy," woke up to his alarm clock at eight o'clock Tuesday evening. After a restful day's sleep, he was now ready for a big night of fighting crime. Gus was (1)_______________ and this gave him an advantage over the other super heroes in his neighborhood, since most criminals did their dirty deeds at night. Gus, in fact, had been (2)______________by the mayor in a warm speech as one of the most helpful super heroes the city ever saw, a (3)_______________ statement since many of the grocers believed that the Sooper Dooper Grocery Guy did more harm than good in their stores. Gus tried not to be (4)______________ about the mayor's compliment, but it was hard, and sometimes the other super heroes found him a little difficult to be around.

Gus put on his tights, cape and T-shirt with a big G on it. He went to the big supermarket on Mason Street and began patrolling the aisles. The night started out slow, and Gus was bored. Nothing was happening in the canned goods aisle, so he wandered over to dairy. Tuesday nights were always slow, but this one seemed (5)_______________ long. Would it ever end? He yearned for some vicious, hardened criminals to fight. He wanted action. He wanted a (6)_______________ night like last Wednesday had been, a night so wild he didn't know if he'd make it out of the grocery store alive.

As Gus sat on the frozen yogurt case recalling last Wednesday's excitement, a chilling scream filled his ears. With Super Dooper quick reactions, Gus ran to the produce section, the source of the scream. There he saw a man running with a little girl tucked under his arm. Jumping to the conclusion that the man was trying to (7)_______________ the little girl, Gus barreled toward him at Super Dooper top speed. "Put that child down, you horrible kidnapper!" he cried. He loved children, and he (8)________________ anyone who tried to hurt them. Gus began throwing heads of lettuce and cabbage and various other green leafy vegetables at the kidnapper. The kidnapper shielded the little girl with his body as he hurled the vegetables back, hard. Gus fell backward into a hard metal shopping cart.

"What do you think you're doing?" the man shouted at Gus. "I'm no kidnapper. I'm her father."

Gus, still in the shopping cart, was stunned, but not silenced. "How can you expect me to believe that, you (9)________________ man? If she's your daughter, then why was she screaming?"

"Someone accidentally ran over her toe with a shopping cart. She was crying because she was hurt. I picked her up to take her home, and we would be there by now if you hadn't started hurling vegetables at us."

"Can't we go home yet, Daddy?" the little girl sobbed.

"Forgive me, sir, for my silly mistake," Gus said in his deepest super hero voice.

As Gus walked home from the grocery store the next morning to go to bed, he decided to go into the (10)_______________ business. Dealing with fabrics had to be easier — and softer — than dealing with shopping carts and heads of lettuce.

Super Challenge

Directions: Use the bonus words from the test to finish the story above.

Vocabulary List #12

aghast: feeling great horror or dismay

- Tiffany was **aghast** to discover she had toilet paper stuck to her shoe while she was being crowned homecoming queen.
- Kate was **aghast** to learn she hadn't made the volleyball team.

redundant: needlessly repetitive

- "Saying *two twins* is **redundant**," said the English teacher.
- "It is important," said Lou's father. "It's vital. It's crucial. It's . . ." He stopped and sighed. "I guess I'm being **redundant**."

gullible: easily fooled or taken in

- Roseanne was so **gullible** she always believed the outlandish stories Maurice told her.
- Sven lost $500 in a telephone scam because he is so **gullible**.

eccentric: out-of-the-ordinary; odd; unconventional

- The **eccentric** woman kept a slice of pepperoni pizza under her mattress in case she got hungry during the night.
- The play is funny because it has so many **eccentric** characters. You never know what they're going to do next.

inanimate: not living

- Shelley didn't think of her stuffed animals as **inanimate** objects. They seemed so alive and real to her.
- A computer is an **inanimate** object, but a hamster is not.

jeer: to make fun of in a rude, sarcastic manner

- When the football team fell behind by another seven points, the fans **jeered** instead of cheered.
- The crowd **jeered** Elaine when her comedy routine flopped.

paradox: a statement that seems inconsistent or contradictory but may be true

- "You say you love him yet hate him," said LuAnn. "That seems like a **paradox** to me."
- "That funny clown is sad," said Craig. "That seems like a **paradox**, but I believe it's true.

ravenous: extremely hungry

- A full day of skiing left Luisa **ravenous**. She ate three plates of spaghetti when she got back to the lodge.
- No matter how much he eats for breakfast, Paul is always **ravenous** by second period.

valiant: brave; courageous

- Even though Wendy didn't win the race, her coach praised her **valiant** effort.
- He was a **valiant** knight who saved damsels in distress.

flourish: to prosper or thrive

- Abe's house plants **flourished** because he took such good care of them.
- Business at the coffee house **flourished** when the owner hired a popular young band.

Bonus Words

★ **mesmerize:** to hypnotize

- Paige sat staring at the TV screen, **mesmerized** by Tom Cruise.
- Blaine's blue eyes can **mesmerize** even the crankiest customer at Hooligan's Market.

★ **destitute:** living in poverty

- The family was **destitute** and had to live in their car.
- Mr. Bandower knew that if he quit his job, his family would be **destitute**.

Name ______________________________

Test

Matching

Match each word in the left column to its correct definition in the right column.

____	1.	flourish	a.	feeling great horror or dismay
____	2.	gullible	b.	to prosper or thrive
____	3.	redundant	c.	a cross between a steer and a jack rabbit
____	4.	paradox	d.	easily fooled or taken in
____	5.	jeer	e.	out-of-the-ordinary; odd; unconventional
____	6.	ravenous	f.	accepting responsibility for an error in judgment
____	7.	aghast	g.	to hypnotize
____	8.	inanimate	h.	living in poverty
____	9.	valiant	i.	a mixture of magenta and lime green
____	10.	eccentric	j.	not living
★ Bonus Words			k.	a statement that seems inconsistent or contradictory but may be true
____	11.	mesmerize	l.	to make fun of in a rude, sarcastic manner
____	12.	destitute	m.	extremely hungry
			n.	needlessly repetitive
			o.	brave; courageous

Fill-in-the-Blank

Directions: The first 10 words listed above belong in the story below. Read the story and use the clues in the text to place each word in the correct blank space provided. You may change the form of a word to fit the story, if you need to. (For example, you might need to add *ed, ing, ly* or *s*.)

Rude Ray Hammers

Becky had hardly eaten a thing all day, so when she got to the party, she was (1)________________. She wanted to head straight for the food table, but Ray Hammers was standing right in front of it. Becky was (2)_______________. How could Ray

Hammers be invited to a party? Nobody even liked him. He was such a pain. If he were just (3)_______________, that would be one thing. She could handle his weird outfits and purple hair. What she didn't like was Ray's behavior. He was really rude. He was always insulting everyone in the class.

She couldn't resist the smell of the popcorn, though, so she walked (4)_______________ across the room looking braver than she felt. She knew Ray would probably start teasing her any second. Sure enough, Ray made a rude comment. "Your hair looks really terrible," he said.

She ignored him.

He continued. "It's sticking straight out in the back."

Becky wasn't (5)_______________. She didn't touch her hair because she knew he was lying.

He continued. "Your hair looks awful. It looks ugly. It looks bad."

Becky looked right at him. "You're being (6)_______________, Ray. Try to be a little more original with your insults."

"You think you are so smart just because you use big words!" he (7)_______________. "Well, you're so smart you are stupid!"

"I think that's called a (8)_______________," said Becky. "It's pretty hard to be smart and stupid at the same time." She tried not to show her annoyance. She wished he were an (9)_______________ object instead of a person who walked and talked. She headed for the popcorn. All she really cared about was getting something to eat.

Ray followed her and watched her get a bowl of popcorn. Without thinking, she handed him a bowl, too.

"No, thanks," he said. "You touched it. I wouldn't eat something you touched."

"Too bad," said Becky. "I've heard that popcorn causes intelligence to (10)_______________. You've probably never tasted it, have you?"

Ray looked puzzled for a moment. Then he grabbed a bowl of popcorn and started off, looking for someone else to bother. Becky just smiled.

Super Challenge

Directions: Use the bonus words from the test to finish the story above.

	1	2	3	4	5	6	7	8
V	taboo	perplexed	nocturnal	flourish	shun	habitually	mesmerize	remorseful
O	abduct	venomous	jeer	consensus	gullible	ravenous	concur	squamulose ★
C	paradox	hotspur ★	infatuated	vivacious	turbulent	amend	gravid ★	haphazard
A	unscrupulous	plectrum ★	persnickety	infinite	howdah ★	tout	mortified	facade
B	filbert ★	ebony	redundant	poltroon ★	succinct	anecdote	vehement	capitulate
R	opaque	loathe	atheist	inanimate	plagiarize	textiles	imperceptible	eccentric
A	valiant	smug	zither ★	guerrilla	destitute	controversial	aghast	vindictive

Vocabulary List #13

synopsis: a summary

- Paula studied for her biology test by reading the chapter **synopsis**. She should have read the chapter instead.
- Ms. Moser was having trouble understanding the plot of the Italian opera, so she read the **synopsis** printed in the program.

idolize: to greatly admire

- Joe **idolized** Michael Jordan and wanted to grow up to be just like him.
- Tiffany **idolized** her older sister and followed her around everywhere she went.

inadvertent: unintentional

- With an **inadvertent** key stroke, Henry deleted his whole term paper from the computer.
- Tasha **inadvertently** put too much butter in her cookies, so they were really greasy.

verify: to prove to be true

- Sometimes, when you order a pizza for delivery, the pizza place will call you back to **verify** that the order is not a prank.
- Shauna said the bank robber had been wearing a red ski mask, and the other witnesses **verified** her statement.

convene: to meet or assemble

- The meeting of Snowboarders for Peace will **convene** at 7:00 PM in the gym.
- The school board **convened** at 6:00 PM and adjourned two hours later.

excerpt: a passage selected from a book, speech, play, film, etc.

- "Mr. Bucco read an **excerpt** from *Huckleberry Finn* that was so interesting it made us want to read the rest of the book," said Clarence, looking surprised.
- The speaker read an **excerpt** from one of Martin Luther King, Jr.'s speeches, and it brought tears to the eyes of the audience.

lucrative: bringing in a lot of money

- Having two paper routes is more **lucrative** than having just one.
- The class fund-raiser was so **lucrative** that the students got to go on a much more expensive class trip than they had expected.

orb: a sphere or circle

- The sun was a glowing orange **orb** rising in the east.
- Eyeballs are **orbs**. So are cantaloupes.

lament: to mourn or grieve

- For months after his family moved to another city, Cory **lamented** the loss of all his friends.
- Long after the funeral, Fawn **lamented** the death of her favorite aunt.

candor: honesty and straightforwardness

- Nina made no excuses to Ross. She told him with **candor** that she simply did not want to go to the prom with him.
- Jane displayed unfortunate **candor** when she told the principal he had bad breath.

Bonus Words

★ **faux:** false; artificial

- My mom refers to her wig as "**faux** hair."
- **Faux** pearls cost less than real ones.

★ **precocious:** smart for his or her age; showing skills or abilities at an earlier age than normal

- Jamal could read when he was only two and a half. He has always been **precocious**.
- Six-year-old Ursula is **precocious**. She already understands calculus.

Name ______________________________

Test

Matching

Match each word in the left column to its correct definition in the right column.

____ 1. synopsis		a.	a summary
____ 2. candor		b.	false; artificial
____ 3. orb		c.	unintentional
____ 4. inadvertent		d.	smart for his or her age; showing skills or abilities at an earlier age than normal
____ 5. verify		e.	type of eyebrow tweezers
____ 6. convene		f.	to prove to be true
____ 7. idolize		g.	to mourn or grieve
____ 8. excerpt		h.	to meet or assemble
____ 9. lucrative		i	space case
____ 10. lament		j.	a passage selected from a book, speech, play, film, etc.
		k.	to greatly admire
		l.	able to leap tall buildings in a single bound
		m.	bringing in a lot of money
		n.	honesty and straightforwardness
		o.	a sphere or circle

★ **Bonus Words**

____ 11. faux

____ 12. precocious

Fill-in-the-Blank

Directions: The first 10 words listed above belong in the story below. Read the story and use the clues in the text to place each word in the correct blank space provided. You may change the form of a word to fit the story, if you need to. (For example, you might need to add *ed, ing, ly* or *s*.)

Fan Club Fanatic

For years, Cali (1)_______________ Denzel Washington. She watched all his movies, stuck posters of him on her walls and (2)_____________ the fact that she lived in Swink, Colorado, instead of Hollywood, where she would have a much better chance of meeting the actor. Not one to be sad for long, though, Cali started a Denzel Washington fan club, whose members (3)_______________ every Friday night to watch the actor's movies and clip (4)_______________ from magazine articles in which he had been mentioned. As the club's president, Cali kept a notebook which contained a (5)_______________of every film Denzel Washington had ever been in.

Cali was normally a very good student, but she threw all her energy into the fan club and (6)______________ let her grades at school slip. Just as she was beginning to bring her grades up and create a balance in her life between school and Denzel, Thad Henderson moved to town and changed everything. Thad was almost as cool as Denzel, almost as cute and had the advantage of being in Cali's homeroom. Cali was determined not let him get away.

As her first step, Cali grabbed all her baby-sitting money and headed down to Francesca's Fortunes and Love Advice. Francesca, a middle-aged woman who looked a lot like Cher, introduced herself with a jewelry-jangling handshake and led Cali into a dark red room. The only light came from an illuminated (7)______________ sitting on a tiny table in the center of the room. "That must be her crystal ball," thought Cali.

After Cali explained her situation, Francesca laid her hands on the crystal ball. "Oh, crystal ball, tell me, will Thad ever return Cali's love?" Lights danced in the crystal ball, and finally Francesca turned to Cali. "Well, honey, I can see that there's no beating around the bush with you. I must speak with (8)______________." Cali held her breath. "The ball says Thad likes you a lot, too."

"Are you sure?" asked Cali. "Can you (9)_____________ that statement by looking again.

Just then a woman appeared in the doorway, and she was dragging Thad Henderson behind her by his ear. "You, Ms. Fortune-teller, are a fraud. I can see by all this expensive stuff that the fortune-telling business must be quite (10)____________, but you're not getting any more of my son's allowance. He may have a crush on some girl named Cali, but that doesn't mean he should be throwing his money away on a fortune-teller."

Right then, Cali knew she wouldn't be spending anymore Friday nights with the Denzel Washington fan club.

Super Challenge

Directions: Use the bonus words from the test to finish the story above.

Vocabulary List #14

seethe: to boil; to be violently agitated or disturbed

- Maggie thought her parents would **seethe** over her cheating. But it was worse than that; they sat quietly and looked very, very disappointed.
- Tony was **seething** inside, but he wasn't about to let Hank know it. He smiled calmly and walked on by.

incompatible: not going together well

- Bonnie and Jeff are **incompatible** on road trips. She likes to stop and look at every attraction, and he hates to get off the highway for any reason at all.
- Alice's boss asked her to transfer to another department because the two of them were so **incompatible**.

paunch: a potbelly

- Ever since he stopped doing his sit-ups, Mr. Romero had been getting a bit of a **paunch**.
- Walt didn't care if he developed a **paunch**. He would never give up his favorite snack of Mountain Dew and Oreos.

proprietor: the owner of a business

- Celestina Monarco became the sole **proprietor** of Monarco's Grocery Store after her husband died.
- If Tom decided to buy the store, he would then become the **proprietor**.

vermin: any of various small, harmful or disgusting animals or insects

- The run-down building was full of **vermin** and quite unsuitable for people to live in.
- If you want to keep your sugar and flour free of **vermin**, store them in the refrigerator.

smitten: struck with a powerful feeling; inspired with love

- Tony was **smitten** with the new girl in his chemistry class. Because he was concentrating on her and not on his Bunsen burner, he knocked it over and burned a hole in the counter.
- Yvonne went to the pool every single day all summer long because she was **smitten** with the lifeguard.

fickle: very changeable in affection, loyalty, etc.

- The **fickle** princess was always changing her mind about which prince she wanted to marry.
- The **fickle** fan always cheered for whichever team was winning.

gaunt: thin and bony

- The artist was **gaunt**. He had been working so hard on his project that he usually forgot to take time to eat.
- Other than looking **gaunt**, the hostage appeared unharmed after being locked up for five days with no food.

meddle: to interfere in someone else's business

- Since Mrs. Busby lives alone, **meddling** in her neighbors' lives makes her own life seem more interesting.
- Mrs. Vance is always snooping around her daughter's room and **meddling** in her personal affairs.

kleptomaniac: someone who is addicted to stealing

- After Kirsten was picked up a fifth time for shoplifting, her parents wondered if maybe she was a **kleptomaniac**.
- When Lila's grandma moved in with her, she had to keep a constant eye on all her things. Her grandma was known for being a **kleptomaniac** who stole salt shakers, pillow cases – anything.

Bonus Words

★ **astute:** clever; intelligent; cunning

- Eleanor was **astute** about investing her money, and she soon became a millionaire.
- "These footprints are muddy. The thief must have come in after it started raining," said the detective, making an observation that wasn't particularly **astute**.

★ **filibuster:** the making of long speeches to prevent a vote on a bill

- The senators kept the **filibuster** going for six days. It's a wonder any of them had a voice left afterwards.
- The 16-hour **filibuster** was successful. It prevented a vote on the bill.

Name ______________________________

Test

Matching

Match each word in the left column to its correct definition in the right column.

____ 1. seethe
____ 2. kleptomaniac
____ 3. meddle
____ 4. gaunt
____ 5. incompatible
____ 6. vermin
____ 7. paunch
____ 8. fickle
____ 9. proprietor
____ 10. smitten

★ Bonus Words

____ 11. filibuster
____ 12. astute

a. to interfere in someone else's business
b. tiny hand warmers
c. thin and bony
d. struck with a powerful feeling; inspired with love
e. not going together well
f. any of various small, harmful or disgusting animals or insects
g. a potbelly
h. the making of long speeches to prevent a vote on a bill
i. the odor of wet wool
j. clever; intelligent; cunning
k. to boil; to be violently agitated or disturbed
l. very changeable in affection, loyalty, etc.
m. a snack made with dill and cucumbers
n. the owner of a business
o. someone who is addicted to stealing

Fill-in-the-Blank

Directions: The first 10 words listed above belong in the story below. Read the story and use the clues in the text to place each word in the correct blank space provided. You may change the form of a word to fit the story, if you need to. (For example, you might need to add *ed, ing, ly* or *s*.)

Coconut Club Chub

Every day after work, Jim stopped at the Coconut Club for a workout. He came so often that the (1)____________ and all the employees knew him by name. Each day he had a new favorite among the exercise machines. He was a (2)____________ man when it came to exercise equipment.

List #14 continued

He hadn't always been an exercise fan. It all started with a comment from his police officer girlfriend Jane, who suggested that maybe Jim was getting a bit of a (3)_________________. "I can't tell from the back, but when I see you from the front, you look a little bit chubby," she said. "It's not a big deal or anything," she added.

Her comments severely wounded Jim. He felt no better than the (4)_____________ that crawled around his kitchen floor, no matter how much he scrubbed it. Then he got angry. "How could Jane say such a thing?" he (5)_________________. Was it true? He stood in front of the mirror for over an hour, examining his figure from every possible angle.

"Who is she to criticize?" he thought. Jane herself wasn't exactly a raving beauty. She could be described as (6)________________, or even scrawny. Jim didn't care. He remained as (7)_______________ with her as he was the day they met.

"Maybe there's more behind Jane's insulting words," Jim worried. "Maybe she thinks we are (8)_______________ and should break up. Or maybe she has no respect for me at all."

He frowned. What if she thought he was no better than Clyde, the local (9)__________________ she had to arrest so often? Jim never could figure that guy out. Why did he keep stealing things he didn't even want?

The next time he saw Jane, Jim persuaded her that she shouldn't (10)______________ in his life by commenting on his stomach. She persuaded Jim that he shouldn't be so sensitive.

The next day, Jim stood in front of his mirror again. After reflecting awhile, he decided to buy a one-month trial membership at the Coconut Club.

Super Challenge

Directions: Use the bonus words from the test to finish the story above.

Vocabulary List #15

veto: to reject

- Theodore had planned on taking his mom's brand new car on his Friday night date, but she **vetoed** that idea.
- The principal informed the student council that she has the power to **veto** any of its decisions if she disagrees with them.

prominent: outstanding; distinguished; readily noticeable

- Brenna's aunt was such a **prominent** lawyer that she didn't even need to advertise.
- Jay Leno has a **prominent** chin.

ethical: moral or right

- "Stealing money from your sister to buy a pack of gum is not **ethical**," said Mrs. Howard.
- Clarisse joined the demonstrators outside the company's walls. "The cruel and painful experiments some companies perform on animals are not **ethical**," she said.

cliché: a stale, over-used expression

- "Quiet as a mouse" is a **cliché**. So is "You can't have your cake and eat it, too."
- Since Harold uses a lot of **clichés**, it is easy to finish his sentences for him.

introvert: a person whose thoughts and interests are directed mostly inward.

- Even though April seemed to be an **introvert**, the drama teacher thought she would be great as the lead in the school play.
- An **introvert** is more likely to prefer writing in a diary to talking on the phone with friends.

extrovert: an outgoing person

- An **extrovert** is more likely to prefer going to a party to writing in his diary.
- Although she liked the **extroverts** in her class very much, the teacher often had to scold them for talking during class.

comprehend: to understand

- "I'll never **comprehend** this algebra lesson," muttered Evelyn, "even if I study it for 20 years!"
- To help his students **comprehend** the workings of a hot air balloon, the professor brought in a diagram.

profound: deep; intense; intelligent

- The editor was hoping to someday receive a book manuscript full of **profound** insight into human nature, but all she ever got was silly fluff.
- Evan expected a **profound** answer when he asked the artist the meaning of her painting, but all she said was, "It's just a painting."

transition: a change

- Nina's mother says lip gloss is the perfect **transition** between wearing no make-up at all and wearing lipstick.
- The **transition** between grade school and junior high is difficult for many students.

simultaneously: happening at the same time

- Brian **simultaneously** talked on the phone and played solitaire on the computer.
- Jonathon was a deep sleeper, so he set six alarm clocks to go off **simultaneously** the morning of his first day of school.

Bonus Words

★ **gobbledygook:** words that are confusing and needlessly official-sounding

- The contract was just a bunch of **gobbledygook** to Tim, so he decided to have his lawyer clarify it for him before he signed.
- Since the politician didn't really know the answer to the reporter's question, he just spoke a lot of **gobbledygook** to try to cover up his ignorance.

★ **carcinogenic:** cancer-causing

- Although cigarettes are **carcinogenic**, many people unwisely smoke them anyway.
- If you're worried about getting cancer, use sunscreen when you're outside. The sun's UV rays are **carcinogenic**.

Name ______________________________

Test

Matching

Match each word in the left column to its correct definition in the right column.

____ 1. cliché
____ 2. veto
____ 3. extrovert
____ 4. simultaneously
____ 5. comprehend
____ 6. transition
____ 7. prominent
____ 8. ethical
____ 9. introvert
____ 10. profound

★ **Bonus Words**

____ 11. gobbledygook
____ 12. carcinogenic

a. happening at the same time
b. a turkey's way of expressing itself
c. outstanding; distinguished; readily noticeable
d. a person whose thoughts and interests are directed mostly inward
e. to reject
f. moral or right
g. an automobile that photographs well in magazines
h. a stale, over-used expression
i. words that are confusing and needlessly official-sounding
j. to understand
k. an outgoing person
l. deep; intense; intelligent
m. cancer-causing
n. a change
o. loose change

Fill-in-the-Blank

Directions: The first 10 words listed above belong in the story below. Read the story and use the clues in the text to place each word in the correct blank space provided. You may change the form of a word to fit the story, if you need to. (For example, you might need to add *ed, ing, ly* or *s*.)

Jackhammer Meeting

The teachers' meeting began promptly at 4:00. (1)__________________, city workers outside began using a jackhammer to repair the street next to the school.

The principal bravely began, despite the noise. She wrote these words on the board: *Look on the bright side.*

"I know these words may be a (2)_______________ that you've all heard before," she said, "but they still help us in our struggle to reach the children of this school."

"Huh?" said Mr. Harrington.

"What?" murmured Miss Moody.

"I CAN'T HEAR YOU!" shouted Mr. Davidson.

The principal bravely carried on, raising her voice. "As the young people in this school struggle to make the (3)_________________ between childhood and adolescence, we must remember to do our best to assist them. We must help both the *A* students and the *F* students. We must help the (4)_________________ as well as the noisier (5)_________________."

"Huh?" shouted Mr. Harrington.

"What?" murmured Miss Moody.

"I CAN'T HEAR YOU!" shouted Mr. Davidson.

Still the principal carried on, raising her voice still higher. "I think we should all remember one of the most (6)_________________ and respected educators of this century, who is remembered for these (7)_________________ words . . ."

"Hold it!" interrupted crabby Miss Moody. "How are we supposed to (8)_________________ what you're trying to say if we can't even hear you? We've got to do something about that noise outside."

"I've got a better idea," yelled Mr. Davidson. "Let's just cancel this meeting!"

The principal immediately (9)________________ the idea. "This is important," she said, giving Mr. Davidson a reprimanding look.

Mr. Davidson had had a very bad day. He was even crankier than usual. "Okay, then," he said. "Let's go pelt the city workers with water balloons until they leave."

The principal was shocked. "Why, Mr. Davidson! That would not be (10)_______________ behavior. It is wrong to hurt other people."

"I thought that would get your attention," he mumbled.

"WHAT?" shouted the principal. "I CAN'T HEAR YOU!"

Super Challenge

Directions: Use the bonus words from the test to finish the story above.

Vocabulary List #16

indignant: angry over something that is mean or unjust

- The Hendersons were **indignant** when the Homeowners Association told them they could not paint their house lime green with electric blue trim.
- When her darling little daughter didn't make the drill team, Frances was **indignant**.

grisly: terrifying; gory; gruesome

- The jury members were terribly upset by the **grisly** pictures of the murder scene.
- Uma picked three **grisly** movies to show at her Halloween party.

consequence: result; outcome; effect

- One **consequence** of not doing your homework is bad grades.
- Sasha suffered the **consequences** of eating too much candy when she had to have six cavities filled.

versatile: adaptable

- Sonya's coat is very **versatile**. She can wear the whole thing on cold days or take the two layers apart and wear only the windbreaker on warmer days.
- Jerry is a **versatile** musician who plays accordion, clarinet, drums and saxophone.

abundant: plentiful; many

- Good food was **abundant** at the Thanksgiving feast.
- The right side of the tree has an **abundance** of berries, but the left side has none.

somber: gloomy; sad

- Lorenzo's mom wouldn't let him paint his room all black because she felt it was too **somber**.
- The **somber** mood at the funeral home made Marjorie even more depressed over the death of her grandmother.

erroneous: mistaken

- The painter made the **erroneous** assumption that the Hudson family wanted their house painted purple.
- Derek **erroneously** believed everyone forgot his 16th birthday. He had no idea his friends had planned a surprise party for him.

pungent: strong, sharp-smelling or tasting

- The diaper pail emitted a **pungent** odor when the lid was opened.
- Rotten fruit produces a **pungent** odor.

secluded: isolated from others

- Thornfield Manor sits on sixteen **secluded** acres. The people who live there rarely run into their neighbors.
- The cabin was completely **secluded**, with no phone, radio or TV. Sandy was miserable.

fiasco: a complete failure

- The school dance turned into a **fiasco** when the sprinkler system accidentally went off and flooded the gymnasium.
- The girls knew the Valentine's party would be a **fiasco** when the only boys who showed up were Joanie's little brothers.

Bonus Words

★translucent: semi-transparent; can be seen through only slightly

- Although Carl could see a figure through the **translucent** curtain, he could not tell who it was.
- Stained glass windows are **translucent**. Regular windows are perfectly clear.

★placate: to do something to make someone stop being angry

- Victor got sick of his mom's complaint that he was never home. He decided to stay home one Saturday evening just to **placate** her.
- For a year Mallory complained about the broken garage door. Finally her husband **placated** her by buying a new one.

Name ______________________________

Test

Matching

Match each word in the left column to its correct definition in the right column.

____ 1. grisly
____ 2. indignant
____ 3. fiasco
____ 4. erroneous
____ 5. pungent
____ 6. consequence
____ 7. secluded
____ 8. abundant
____ 9. somber
____ 10. versatile

★Bonus Words
____ 11. translucent
____ 12. placate

a. semi-transparent; can be seen through only slightly
b. strong, sharp-smelling or tasting
c. a huge and powerful kind of bear
d. terrifying; gory; gruesome
e. result; outcome; effect
f. to do something to make someone stop being angry
g. adaptable
h. plentiful; many
i. a non-dairy shake
j. gloomy; sad
k. angry over something that is mean or unjust
l. to squint
m. mistaken
n. isolated from others
o. a complete failure

Fill-in-the-Blank

Directions: The first 10 words listed above belong in the story below. Read the story and use the clues in the text to place each word in the correct blank space provided. You may change the form of a word to fit the story, if you need to. (For example, you might need to add *ed, ing, ly* or *s.*)

Ax Murderers and Ghosts

It was a dark and stormy night. Still, Emily and her friends decided to continue their plan to explore the old house on the next block, the house everyone said was haunted.

Emily had her doubts. "What if it *is* haunted?" she asked. "Going inside could have terrible (1)______________. The ghosts, or whatever they are, might kill us, chop us into little pieces or worse."

"What could be worse than being chopped up in little pieces?" asked Dirk. "You always have such (2)_____________ thoughts!"

"I do not!" said Emily, looking (3)________________. She scowled at him.

"I don't think ghosts have to be nasty," said Dirk. "They could be friendly, happy ghosts. They could be very (4)_____________ and sing and dance and play musical instruments."

"Or they could be funny ghosts," added Spencer. "My sister told me about a ghost who played practical jokes on a family. Once when they sat down to dinner, the roasted chicken the mother took out of the oven turned out to be a roasted rat. It had such a (5)_______________ odor that everyone left the room gagging."

"That's supposed to be funny?" said Emily, shuddering.

"It's not funny," said Jeanetta. "But it's ridiculous. If you think that ghosts exist, you are making an (6)_______________ assumption. They don't exist. When we go into the house, we might meet spiders or rats or serial killers or ax murderers — but not any ghosts."

"How comforting," said Emily sarcastically.

"I guess that running into an ax murderer could turn an adventure into a (7)________________," admitted Jeanetta.

"But running into rats would be exciting," said Spencer. "I think rats are fascinating. One or two rats would be interesting, but what I'd really like to see is an (8)_________________ supply of rats in the house."

"You are a sick person," said Emily. "You should stay in a (9)_______________ place away from other human beings. That way we won't catch whatever is wrong with you."

"Look, if we're going to go, let's go," Dirk interrupted.

Suddenly, everyone was quiet. The mood in the room was (10)____________ as they listened to the thunder and thought about ax murderers and rats and ghosts. Everyone waited for someone else to move.

No one did.

Super Challenge

Directions: Use the bonus words from the test to finish the story above.

	1	2	3	4	5	6	7	8
V	smitten	orb	galluses ★	incompatible	pugilist ★	verify	filibuster	transition
O	consequence	veto	secluded	fiasco	precocious	extrovert	synopsis	cliché
C	faux	profound	proprietor	idolize	plinth ★	gaunt	catamount ★	pungent
A	erroneous	inadvertent	translucent	ethical	seethe	indignant	kleptomaniac	lucrative
B	prominent	versatile	excerpt	comprehend	astute	spoonerism ★	paunch	fickle
R	convene	gobbledygook	somber	vermin	jape ★	candor	introvert	grisly
A	abundant	meddle	chernozem ★	lament	simultaneously	knout ★	placate	carcinogenic

Vocabulary List #17

morale: the state of a group's or a person's spirits

- The football team's **morale** was sinking, so the cheerleaders did several more cheers than they had planned.
- **Morale** was low in algebra class. Instead of explaining what they did wrong and showing them the right way to solve an equation, Mrs. Stojak just gave everyone an *F*.

sarcastic: said in a sneering or mocking way, often indicating the opposite of what is obvious

- "Yeah, you're real tough, aren't you?" said the bully in a **sarcastic** tone to his latest victim, who was lying on the ground with a bloody nose.
- When Liza returned the sweater she borrowed from Erin with a hole in it, Erin said **sarcastically**, "Thanks a lot!"

vice: a shortcoming; an immoral habit

- Nan's Grandpa Dominic eats well, gets plenty of sleep and doesn't drink. His only **vice** is smoking cigars.
- "My biggest **vice** is eating too much chocolate," said Morris.

contempt: scorn; dislike

- Amy expressed her dislike of the new mayor in a letter filled with **contempt** to the city council.
- To show his **contempt** for all people who didn't speak at least three languages, Mr. Dunn yelled at them in one of the languages they didn't know.

virtuoso: someone who shows great technical skill in some fine art, especially music

- Georgia was such a **virtuoso** on the fiddle that she joined a bluegrass band when she was only 13.
- Picasso was a **virtuoso** with a paintbrush.

oblivious: unaware

- As she dripped ice cream all over her face, Janie's little sister just smiled, **oblivious** to the bumble bee circling her head.
- Mr. Ricken continued his boring lecture, **oblivious** to the fact that half the class was falling asleep.

apprehend: to capture

- The thief ran fast, but the police officer ran faster and was able to **apprehend** him.
- Jarrod couldn't figure out how to **apprehend** the person who was stealing from his locker.

terrain: ground

- The **terrain** was so rough that Adrienne couldn't hike it in her new high heels.
- The scientists tried to build a robot that could move around on the rocky **terrain** of the moon without tipping over.

diligent: careful and hard-working

- Rachel was **diligent** about practicing the tuba. Her brother was **diligent** about stuffing his ears with cotton before she started.
- Loralee **diligently** did her homework every night for a week. Then she decided she liked watching TV more than studying.

prudent: exercising good judgment or common sense

- It is not **prudent** to put off your homework on the chance that we might get five feet of snow and not have to go to school tomorrow.
- Dylan's new friends wanted him to ignore his curfew. No matter how much he wanted to fit in, he didn't think it was **prudent** to follow their advice.

Bonus Words

★ **extemporaneous:** impromptu; done or spoken with little preparation

- Patrick launched into an **extemporaneous** explanation of what he had seen at the museum. Although he hadn't taken notes or planned a speech, he did a good job.
- Tim wasn't good at **extemporaneous** speeches. But when he had time to prepare and rehearse, he was the best in class.

★ **altruistic:** unselfishly interested in the welfare of others

- Mother Theresa was known as an **altruistic** person because of all the time she devoted to helping the needy.
- Not all volunteers are **altruistic**. Some just want to beef up their resumés or get their picture in the paper.

Name ______________________________

Test

Matching

Match each word in the left column to its correct definition in the right column.

____ 1. oblivious
____ 2. diligent
____ 3. morale
____ 4. prudent
____ 5. virtuoso
____ 6. terrain
____ 7. apprehend
____ 8. contempt
____ 9. vice
____ 10. sarcastic

★Bonus Words

____ 11. extemporaneous
____ 12. altruistic

a. exercising good judgment or common sense
b. exercising to impress the girl you like in math class
c. unselfishly interested in the welfare of others
d. said in a sneering or mocking way, often indicating the opposite of what is obvious
e. a shortcoming; an immoral habit
f. the state of a group's or a person's spirits
g. scorn; dislike
h. the inability to eat food that is green
i.. someone who shows great technical skill in some fine art, especially music
j. to capture
k. unaware
l. ground
m. grounded for two whole weeks
n. careful and hard-working
o. impromptu; done or spoken with little preparation

Fill-in-the-Blank

Directions: The first 10 words listed above belong in the story below. Read the story and use the clues in the text to place each word in the correct blank space provided. You may change the form of a word to fit the story, if you need to. (For example, you might need to add *ed, ing, ly* or *s.)*

The Trouble with Brothers

Rachel hated this time of year. Every April, Ms. Chen held a piano recital and made all her students play at least one piece in it. Every year, Rachel's little brother Mozy (short for Mozart, of course) picked the hardest piece of music he could find and played it perfectly. The little boy was truly a (1)______________ when it came to the piano, and it didn't hurt

List #17 continued

that he was (2)_______________ about practicing. For three hours every day — rain, snow, or shine — Mozy played his songs and practiced his scales. The kid was so focused on his music that he seemed (3)_______________ to the world around him.

Rachel, on the other hand, spent the rainy days splashing in puddles and the sunny days expertly riding her mountain bike over the rocky, rough (4)_______________ of the nearby foothills. She made up stories as she rode. Sometimes she pretended she was chasing down a dangerous fugitive of the law, whose (5)_______________ was robbing banks. But every time she was just about to (6)_______________ the imaginary outlaw and bring him back to jail, she would hear her very real mother calling her to come home and get ready for her piano lesson. "Oh, I can hardly wait," she always wanted to say. She knew, though, that it wouldn't be (7)_______________ to make such a (8)_________________ remark to her mother, who would ground her in a flash, and then she would *never* get away from Mozy's playing.

Actually, she liked her little brother quite a bit, and sometimes he could even be sort of fun to be around. However, every day during the three hour piano practice marathon, she felt nothing but (9)_________________ for the little runt. He made her look bad. She couldn't even have her friends over for a game of basketball in the driveway. By the time she got everyone organized into teams, Mozy's beautiful but depressing music would drift outside and sink her friends' (10)_______________, making them feel so sad that they wanted to go home. Rachel wanted to strangle him.

Later, when it came time for the recital, he played perfectly. Then Rachel was the one who was depressed. She *didn't* play perfectly.

Super Challenge

Directions: Use the bonus words from the test to finish the story above.

Vocabulary List #18

subsequent: coming after; following in time, place or order

- Because she did such a great job baby-sitting the Davis children, Maria was asked back to baby-sit each **subsequent** Saturday.
- Catherine committed a technical foul at the end of the game, so her coach benched her for three **subsequent** games.

facsimile: an exact copy or reproduction

- Using some aluminum pipe and scrap metal he found in the garage, Ryan created a miniature **facsimile** of the jumbo jet.
- Katrina's bracelet was a cheap **facsimile** of the expensive one Penny owned.

retrieve: to get something back

- With a piece of gum and a string, Emma was able to **retrieve** her earring when it fell down the drain.
- Most dogs can learn to **retrieve** a Frisbee if you teach them when they are puppies.

engrossed: totally absorbed in

- The teacher and principal were so **engrossed** in a conversation about Carl's falling grades that they barely heard the sirens outside.
- Margaret was so **engrossed** in her soap opera that she left her noodles boiling until they stuck to the pot.

concise: brief and to the point

- "Don't give me a 10-minute speech about this," said the principal. "I just want a **concise** explanation of your behavior."
- **Concise** writing is good writing. A lot of extra words clutter your sentences and muddle your meaning.

fortnight: two weeks

- Crystal planned to be gone a **fortnight**. She would miss classes for 10 full days.
- A typical year is made up of 26 **fortnights**.

mediate: to settle a dispute between two opposing sides

- When the baseball players went on strike, someone was called in to **mediate** the dispute.
- The baby-sitter found herself forever **mediating** the children's arguments.

corpulent: fat

- He was a **corpulent** boy who loved potato chips and hot fudge sundaes with pecans and whipped cream.
- Santa Claus is a **corpulent** man with rosy cheeks and sparkling eyes.

bravado: false, showy bravery

- J.J. strutted up to the lion with a lot of **bravado**, but as soon as the animal opened his mouth to yawn, J.J. ran away at full speed.
- Achilles marched onto the field with such **bravado** that all the other warriors were frightened.

terrorism: use of terror or violence as a means of getting what you want

- To discourage **terrorism**, security guards patrolled the airport 24 hours a day.
- **Terrorism** struck Oklahoma City when the federal building was blown up.

Bonus Words

★despondent: dejected; hopeless

- After failing her driver's test three times, Charlotte grew **despondent** and didn't want to practice anymore.
- Whitney was **despondent** over her break-up with Charlie — until Corrine brought over half a gallon of ice cream and her handsome cousin Luke.

★albatross: a burden

- Carlos finally quit the debate team. It took so much time it had become an **albatross**.
- Sponsoring student council, with all the phone calls, elections and arguments that it required, had become such an **albatross** that Mr. Miller finally quit.

List #18

Name ______________________

Test

Matching

Match each word in the left column to its correct definition in the right column.

____ 1. corpulent
____ 2. bravado
____ 3. facsimile
____ 4. engrossed
____ 5. concise
____ 6. fortnight
____ 7. mediate
____ 8. subsequent
____ 9. retrieve
____ 10. terrorism

★**Bonus Words**

____ 11. despondent
____ 12. albatross

a. to get something back
b. totally absorbed in
c. wicked
d. brief and to the point
e. to settle a dispute between two opposing sides
f. coming after; following in time, place, or order
g. the face you make when you bite your tongue
h. an exact copy or reproduction
i. a burden
j. fat
k. false, showy bravery
l. use of terror or violence as a means of getting what you want
m any of various appliances used for toasting bread
n. two weeks
o. dejected; hopeless

Fill-in-the-Blank

Directions: The first 10 words listed above belong in the story below. Read the story and use the clues in the text to place each word in the correct blank space provided. You may change the form of a word to fit the story, if you need to. (For example, you might need to add *ed, ing, ly* or *s.)*

The Something War Somewhere

"What did you learn in school today?" asked Dad.

"Nothing," mumbled Max.

"Nothing?" asked Dad. "NOTHING?"

"Nothing much," added Max.

"If you learned nothing much, you weren't doing what you were supposed to be doing. I think you should stay home this weekend and study."

"Oh," said Max. "Let me rethink that answer."

"Good idea," said Dad. "I'm listening . . ."

"Okay. First my history teacher talked about current events. He said that some people in some country somewhere committed an act of (1)_______________ to get something they wanted. They acted with (2)_________________, but my teacher said they were really cowards . . . I'm worried about him, by the way."

"About who?"

"My history teacher. He's been looking too thin lately, and he used to be so (3)_______________ that he had trouble getting his jacket buttoned."

"It's kind of you to be so concerned," said Dad, "but go on with current events. Describe the (4)______________ actions of the people you were describing in the country somewhere. What did they do next?"

"Well, they sent a letter. I remember that. And they made a (5)______________ of the letter and sent it somewhere else, too. I think it was to another country."

"Then what happened?"

"I guess I got so (6)_________________ in trying to figure out why Mr. Zylstra was losing weight that I didn't quite catch everything."

"Tell me what you remember."

"Mr. Zylstra said somebody tried to help settle the dispute between the people in the first country and whoever it was they were mad at. Then there was an explosion. It was just like another explosion that had happened a (7)______________ earlier. Everyone was outraged, so the attempt to (8)_______________ the dispute failed."

"Where was the explosion?"

"Um . . ." Max closed his eyes and frowned. "I'm trying to (9)______________ that information."

Dad waited.

"I can't remember," said Max.

"When is your test on this?"

"Next week. It's supposed to be an essay test."

"Well, with what you know about this subject, your answers will be very (10)_______________," said Dad, sighing.

Super Challenge

Directions: Use the bonus words from the test to finish the story above.

____

____

____

____

____

____

____

____

____

____

____

____

____

Vocabulary List #19

quibble: to argue over picky, unimportant details

- "I don't mean to **quibble**," said Jane, "but don't you think violet would be a better color for that poster than lavender?"
- The committee members didn't get anything accomplished because they spent all their time **quibbling** over who would get the last cream puff.

malady: illness; disease

- Isabelle was disappointed when her doctor told her that her **malady** would keep her from attending Brenda's 16th birthday party.
- Don's **malady** made him tired and achy.

condone: to forgive or overlook

- The landlord warned his new tenants that he did not **condone** loud parties.
- The substitute teacher **condoned** talking during the test, so—not surprisingly — everyone had the same answers to the test questions.

sentimental: very emotional (sometimes overly so)

- Elsa is so **sentimental** she cries just thinking about the movie *E.T.*
- The necklace held **sentimental** value for Tess. It was a gift from her grandmother.

obstinate: stubborn

- The **obstinate** child refused to put her toys away, even after being asked four times to do so.
- Greg and Gina's argument will never be resolved because they are both so **obstinate**.

tangible: real; actual; capable of being touched

- Opal broke up with Bill because all he ever did was *say* he loved her. She wanted something more **tangible**, like a diamond ring.
- Isaac liked the respect he received at work, but he also enjoyed the more **tangible** rewards, like money.

profit: gain; benefit

- Before she went to jail, Tanya made money by stealing things and then selling them for a **profit**.
- "How can we make a **profit** if we sell the machine for less than it cost to make it?" asked the frustrated business owner.

innovation: a new idea or way of doing things

- E-mail is an **innovation** that has made writing letters to people a lot less trouble than it used to be.
- Linda's **innovation** changed the rubber band industry forever.

replenish: to fill again

- The cowboys stopped at the stream to **replenish** their water supply.
- Ms. Malone got up three times during supper to **replenish** the bowl of delicious mashed potatoes.

irrelevant: off the subject; unimportant

- The history teacher's stories about his two-year-old son were completely **irrelevant** to the discussion the class was trying to have about World War II.
- Mean Mr. Stanton told Shannon, "The fact that your house burned down last night is **irrelevant**. You should always have your homework done when you come to class."

Bonus Words

★chastise: to punish; to discipline

- After the jury found her guilty of burglary, the defendant was **chastised** severely by the judge, who sentenced her to two years in jail.
- Mr. Plambeck **chastised** his daughters for giggling during the sermon. "Reverend Adams couldn't help it if his toupee slipped," he said sternly.

★countenance: facial expression

- Jacey didn't say a word, but her **countenance** revealed her true feelings for Martin.
- Gary peeked at Shari from the window, and she could tell from his **countenance** that he was scared.

Name ____________________________

Test

Matching

Match each word in the left column to its correct definition in the right column.

____ 1. condone	a.	a cross between an orange and a nectarine
____ 2. irrelevant	b.	to forgive or overlook
____ 3. obstinate	c.	very emotional (sometimes overly so)
____ 4. tangible	d.	illness; disease
____ 5. replenish	e.	an Elvis Presley sighting
____ 6. profit	f.	real; actual; capable of being touched
____ 7. sentimental	g.	gain; benefit
____ 8. innovation	h.	to punish; to discipline
____ 9. malady	i.	a new idea or way of doing things
____ 10. quibble	j.	to fill again
★Bonus Words	k.	what they used to call women in medieval times
____ 11. countenance	l.	off the subject; unimportant
____ 12. chastise	m.	stubborn
	n.	to argue over picky, unimportant details
	o.	facial expression

Fill-in-the-Blank

Directions: The first 10 words listed above belong in the story below. Read the story and use the clues in the text to place each word in the correct blank space provided. You may change the form of a word to fit the story, if you need to. (For example, you might need to add *ed, ing, ly* or *s*.)

The Electric Automatic Toilet Paper Unwinder

Professor Nancy McDougal had spent the last seven days and nights in her lab trying to perfect her invention, an electric automatic toilet paper unwinder. Although she spent much of her career working on theories, this invention was something (1)________________, something she could see and touch, something she could sell. She believed with all her heart that her invention was a true (2)_______________ in the world of toilet paper. She believed it would change the world's restroom experiences forever.

Whenever she imagined her electric automatic toilet paper unwinder, she got tears in her eyes, and she was normally not a very (3)_______________ person. She also grew very emotional when she thought about all the money her invention would make. She planned to sell it for five times the amount it cost to build. That would give her a huge (4)_____________.

Tears were welling up again in Professor McDougal's eyes when a loud knock came at the door of her lab. "Nancy, Nancy? Are you in there? Are you still working on that silly toilet paper thing?" It was her husband. Roger was ordinarily very supportive of her work, but he really wasn't very interested in the electric automatic toilet paper unwinder.

"Nancy, at least come out and eat dinner," he said, jiggling the locked door. "Please, honey, don't be (5)_______________. I've asked you three times today to come out and eat. The children are beginning to worry that you're suffering from some (6)_______________. At least show them you're all right."

Finally, Professor McDougal tore herself away from her work and came down to dinner.

"Roger, you knocked on my door and interrupted my work four times today, and that is something I just won't (7)_____________. If you keep this up, I'll have to rent that old building downtown and set up my lab there."

"I don't want to (8)_____________," Roger replied, "but it was *three*, not four, times that I knocked on the door and interrupted you."

Nancy couldn't let that go. "The number of times you knocked on my door is (9)_____________. The point is that you interrupted me while I was working."

Roger and Nancy realized that they had a few problems to work out with one another.

After a long discussion, they found a way to compromise. She would work less in her lab, but when she was there, Roger wouldn't interrupt her.

The electric automatic toilet paper unwinder was a big success, and Roger and Nancy used the money to (10)______________ their savings account, which had been nearly emptied the year before when they started paying for their daughter's college education. The University of Electromagnetic Engineering was not a cheap school.

Super Challenge

Directions: Use the bonus words from the test to finish the story above.

____

____

____

____

____

____

____

____

____

____

____

____

____

____

____

Vocabulary List #20

dupe: to fool, trick or cheat someone

- Lyle was **duped** into thinking he would make thousands of dollars in a week just by selling banana-flavored bubble gum to little kids.
- Morgan **duped** his older sister into letting him go along to the mall by pretending their mother had asked him to buy something for her there.

cantankerous: quarrelsome

- Sonya hoped her grandfather would be nicer and more patient after he married Patsy, but she was wrong. He was as **cantankerous** as ever.
- Although the new mayor was **cantankerous**, the committee members still hoped they could reach some agreement with him.

insolent: boldly disrespectful and arrogant

- Sara's nephew was so **insolent** that she hated visiting her sister when he was around.
- Mrs. Tucker was the first teacher to stand up to the bully's **insolent** behavior.

coddle: to pamper or protect too much

- "Terrell's mom **coddles** him too much," said Carolyn. "He's such a mamma's boy!"
- "We don't **coddle** our recruits!" shouted the drill sergeant. "I don't care if you have an ingrown toenail! Get in line!"

reciprocate: to return a favor or feeling

- After Emilio threw her a party, Lindy felt she should **reciprocate**, so she took him out to dinner.
- Bumble the clown landed a punch. His partner **reciprocated** by snapping Bumble's suspenders so hard he fell over.

verbatim: exactly word for word

- Meg got an *F* on her research paper because the teacher discovered she had copied it **verbatim** from the encyclopedia.
- "The speaker used my words **verbatim** and didn't even give me credit!" complained Sue.

diffuse: to spread out

- The light above the table was too bright and harsh. Monica wished she could **diffuse** it so her eyes wouldn't get so tired.
- When the hazardous chemicals expert opened the canister, the gas **diffused** through the room.

peal: a loud sound

- A **peal** of laughter filled the room when the comedian made his Jaba the Hut face.
- When it turned midnight on New Year's Eve, there was a **peal** from the bell at St. Bernadette's Church.

interval: space or time between two items or events

- A football field is marked with a white chalky powder at ten-yard **intervals**.
- "The **interval** between bells is too long," sighed David as he sat through another endless biology class.

abhor: to hate or detest

- "I **abhor** Coke, ice cream and pizza," said Missy. "I guess I'm not normal."
- Bonnie **abhors** spiders and faints at the sight of them.

Bonus Words

★innate: having ever since birth; not learned

- Jamie's high self-esteem is **innate**. She was confident even as a baby.
- Since both his parents were artists, Sean has an **innate** talent for drawing.

★omnipotent: all-powerful

- The dictator believed he was **omnipotent** — until he was overthrown.
- "Around our house, my parents are **omnipotent**," said Jo Lynn. "What they say goes."

Name ______________________________

Test

Matching

Match each word in the left column to its correct definition in the right column.

____ 1. cantankerous
____ 2. interval
____ 3. insolent
____ 4. coddle
____ 5. reciprocate
____ 6. dupe
____ 7. verbatim
____ 8. diffuse
____ 9. peal
____ 10. abhor

★Bonus Words

____ 11. innate
____ 12. omnipotent

a. having ever since birth; not learned
b. to fool, trick or cheat someone
c. all-powerful
d. a loud sound
e. unable to concentrate during vocabulary tests
f. to hate or detest
g. quarrelsome
h. boldly disrespectful and arrogant
i. exactly word for word
j. to return a favor or feeling
k. to pamper or protect too much
l. a kind of diaper
m. space or time between two items or events
n. to spread out
o. a breed of small domestic chicken

Fill-in-the-Blank

Directions: The first 10 words listed above belong in the story below. Read the story and use the clues in the text to place each word in the correct blank space provided. You may change the form of a word to fit the story, if you need to. (For example, you might need to add *ed, ing, ly* or *s.)*

The Lifeguard and the Chocolate Syrup

Travis did not like being a lifeguard. It was hot and boring work. He was always (1)________________ when he got home at night, picking arguments with both his sisters.

Billy Rogers was the eight-year-old who plagued Travis daily with his obnoxious behavior at the pool. Billy's parents had (2)______________ him all his life, letting him have his way about everything. Travis had spent his whole summer yelling at Billy at one-hour (3) ________________. "Billy! No dunking people," he would shout.

Then, "Billy! No running!"

Or "Billy! No throwing dirt into the pool."

Thanks to Billy, Travis knew the official pool rule book (4) ________________. It seemed that he recited most of it to Billy every single day.

One day late in August, Billy decided to pour 13 gallons of chocolate syrup into the pool. He expected a (5)________________ of laughter from everyone watching. Instead, after taking one look at the angry glare on Travis' face, everyone in the stands and in the pool grew completely silent.

"Billy Rogers! Report to the lifeguard stand immediately," Travis thundered through the megaphone he had used so often that summer. The (6)________________ little boy just laughed scornfully at the lifeguard, climbed the steps to the low dive, poured in five more gallons of syrup and watched as it (7)________________ through the water and down to the shallow end. As he picked up another gallon of syrup, Billy found himself staring up at Travis, who had decided it was time to (8)________________.

Holding Billy tightly by the arm, Travis picked up the remaining gallon and began to pour the chocolate syrup slowly over Billy's head. Everyone cheered. Although Travis knew he would take some heat for making the little boy such a sticky mess, he felt a lot better about his career as a lifeguard. (Later, of course, Billy tried to (9)________________ his parents into thinking that he'd had nothing to do with the chocolate in the swimming pool.)

The following summer, when he was contentedly making chocolate sundaes at the Tasty Freeze, Travis could honestly say he no longer (10)______________ Billy. Just remembering the sticky mess made him smile and think more kindly of the kid.

Super Challenge

Directions: Use the bonus words from the test to finish the story above.

	1	2	3	4	5	6	7	8
V	morale	mediate	sentimental	subsequent	insolent	replenish	prudent	irrelevant
O	extemporaneous	scimitar ★	peal	quibble	vice	profit	bravado	innate
C	chastise	reciprocate	sarcastic	despondent	quoit ★	engrossed	condone	oblivious
A	retrieve	corpulent	rococo ★	dupe	altruistic	cantankerous	verbatim	malady
B	innovation	apprehend	interval	terrorism	yegg ★	contempt	tsunami ★	concise
R	terrain	diffuse	williwaw ★	diligent	coddle	facsimile	omnipotent	tangible
A	abhor	xenophobia ★	virtuoso	albatross	obstinate	curlew ★	fortnight	countenance

Vocabulary List #21

abolish: to do away with

- The student council hopes to **abolish** the school rule against holding hands in the hallway. The members think holding hands is fine.
- Poor Mrs. Stafford wished that bubble gum could be **abolished** so she would never again have to find a wad of it stuck to the desks.

qualms: feelings of uneasiness or doubt

- "Do you have any **qualms** about the ski trip this weekend, or do you think everything will be all right?" asked Kim.
- Sandy had **qualms** about letting Shane copy her homework, but she liked him so much she let him do it anyway.

coincidental: happening by chance

- "Surely it wasn't **coincidental** that my diary disappeared the night I caught you snooping in my room," Alissa said to her brother.
- It was not **coincidental** that Laurel ran into Tyler at the mall. Her best friend told her he would be there.

benevolent: kind

- Even though Alfred won the lottery, he didn't lose his **benevolent** spirit. He still volunteered at the soup kitchen and took in stray animals.
- "You are truly a **benevolent** woman, Ms. Stanley," said the orphanage director as he accepted her large donation.

futile: useless; in vain

- Jay's attempts to lose weight were **futile**. He just kept gaining and gaining.
- After a full year of trying to get her students to turn in their homework on time, Miss Craig decided her efforts were **futile** and just gave up.

ludicrous: laughable; absurd

- Harlan thought the idea of holding the prom in a gas station parking lot was **ludicrous**, but he was polite and listened to the idea anyway.
- Juliet warned her younger sister that it was **ludicrous** to expect their parents to let her stay out until midnight on a school night.

ambrosia: food of the gods in Greek and Roman mythology; something that tastes or smells really delicious

- "Ah, **ambrosia**!" sighed the food critic, taking another bite of the restaurant's specialty.
- Zeus and Apollo finished off their **ambrosia** with a gallon of sweet nectar.

incensed: angry; enraged

- Nick's refusal to go to college **incensed** his father.
- Mrs. Vance was **incensed** when she saw green chili all over the white sweater she had loaned her daughter.

stringent: severe; strict

- Lindsey's parents set **stringent** rules. She has to be home by 5:00 PM every night and finish her homework by 8:00 PM.
- John was on a **stringent** diet that allowed him only one snack food a week.

coalition: a union, group or alliance

- A **coalition** of school, religious and community groups fought the proposed amendment.
- Mr. Baker knew he couldn't fight the school board on his own, so he formed a **coalition** of teachers who shared his opinion.

Bonus Words

★ **vicariously:** through someone else, as in experiencing something by imagined participation in someone else's experience

- Gabby's Aunt Rita is so addicted to her soap operas that she has begun to live **vicariously** through the characters.
- **Vicariously**, through his quarterback son, Mr. Hooper lived out his dream of being a football star.

★ **ruminate:** to think about or to meditate on

- The boys didn't have a car for their big date. "Let's **ruminate** for a while," said Joseph. "I'll bet we can find a solution."
- Newton was sitting under a tree **ruminating** about the problem of gravity when an apple fell on his head.

Name ______________________________

Test

Matching

Match each word in the left column to its correct definition in the right column.

____ 1. abolish
____ 2. ambrosia
____ 3. stringent
____ 4. ludicrous
____ 5. qualms
____ 6. coalition
____ 7. benevolent
____ 8. futile
____ 9. incensed
____ 10. coincidental

★Bonus Words

____ 11. vicariously
____ 12. ruminate

a. happening by chance
b. to do away with
c. any whole number divisible by 12
d. food of the gods in Greek and Roman mythology; something that tastes or smells really delicious
e. a union, group or alliance
f. useless; in vain
g. in pain
h. to think about or to meditate on
i. angry; enraged
j. feelings of uneasiness or doubt
k. the compression of clowns in a Volkswagen Bug
l. severe; strict
m. laughable; absurd
n. through someone else, as in experiencing something by imagined participation in someone else's experience
o. kind

Fill-in-the-Blank

Directions: The first 10 words listed above belong in the story below. Read the story and use the clues in the text to place each word in the correct blank space provided. You may change the form of a word to fit the story, if you need to. (For example, you might need to add *ed, ing, ly* or *s.)*

Last Quack Duck Head Pie

Chef school turned out to be harder than Anthony had expected, but he loved it anyway. He loved the challenge of learning about all the different spices, meats and doughs. He even excelled, despite the very (1)______________ rules that caused many students to drop out. He did so well in his Desserts of the World class that he came up with a dessert so delicious his teacher compared it to (2)______________.

During his last year of chef school, Anthony had to prepare a final meal that would determine whether or not he graduated. There was a catch though— the final meal had to include a dish called Last Quack Duck Head Pie. The name was so (3)________________ that Anthony thought it was a joke. Unfortunately, it wasn't.

"I can't prepare anything called Last Quack Duck Head Pie!" exclaimed Anthony.

"You will prepare it, or you will fail chef school!" cried Anthony's instructor. He was (4)________________ at Anthony's remark. He was so angry his face turned a brilliant shade of red.

Anthony knew arguing with his instructor was (5)________________. He absolutely had to figure out how to make Last Quack Duck Head Pie, or he would fail the test and not graduate.

On the day of his meal preparing exam, Anthony stood before his table and sighed heavily. He had many (6)________________ about the meal. He doubted that he could do it. He loved ducks and didn't see how he could put one in a pie.

Anthony glanced over at the student next to him. She, too, was supposed to prepare Last Quack Duck Head Pie. Anthony noticed that her complexion was green and he feared she might faint.

"Are you okay?" he asked the woman.

"No, I'm not. The idea of preparing this meal is making me sick to my stomach. I guess I'm just too (7)________________. I can't imagine putting a little duckie in a pie, even if it means flunking chef school."

"I can't either," said Anthony. "I love ducks. You know, we should form a (8)________________ and refuse to make Last Quack Duck Head Pie. Maybe we could even get this ridiculous meal (9)________________ as part of our final exam."

In only a few minutes, Anthony and the woman convinced all the other students to rebel with them. Soon the students were releasing ducks all over the city, saving hundreds of lives. Not liking the bad publicity over the inhumane dish, the dean of the school quickly cut Last Quack Duck Head Pie from the school's curriculum.

After graduating from chef school, Anthony started a duck rescue program. He worked at the duck shelter in the mornings, before he went to work at a restaurant. It may have been (10)________________, but most of the ducks arrived at the shelter when Anthony was working. He liked to think they had heard about his efforts on their behalf and wanted to meet him.

Super Challenge

Directions: Use the bonus words from the test to finish the story above.

____

____

____

____

____

____

____

____

____

____

____

____

Vocabulary List #22

coagulate: to clot

- If your blood doesn't **coagulate** when you cut yourself, you could bleed to death.
- The grease **coagulated** in the jar, forming a solid whitish lump that smelled bad.

equitable: fair to all concerned

- The jury decided on an **equitable** settlement for Jonathan, who was injured when the plant exploded.
- When two children fight over a toy, the only **equitable** solution is to take the toy away completely and let them both be unhappy.

obsolete: no longer in use or in fashion

- Natalie's dad loves his old eight-track tape player, even though he knows it is **obsolete**.
- The word used in the old manuscript was **obsolete**, so no one knew quite what it meant.

belligerent: showing a readiness to argue or quarrel

- "It's because you're so **belligerent** that we argue all the time," said Marcie.
- "Maybe you would get along with people better if you weren't so **belligerent** every time anyone has the least little criticism of your work," said Hank's boss.

candid: open and honest

- "I'll be **candid** with you, Calvin," said Mr. Silverstein. "The reason you flunked is because you never did any work."
- Jenni was **candid** with Tom about his bad breath. She told him to brush his teeth after every meal and to stop eating so much garlic.

infallible: incapable of error; never wrong

- Zelda seemed to think she was **infallible**, even though just last week she missed a word on her spelling test.
- "Okay, I marked your test incorrectly," apologized Mr. Kline. "I'm not **infallible**, you know."

acronym: a word formed from the first letters of several other words

- S.A.D.D. is an **acronym** for Students Against Drunk Driving.
- H.E.L.P. is an **acronym** for Haybailers Eating Lemon Pies.

substantial: considerable; large; significant

- Maria saved a **substantial** amount of money by buying only clothes that were on sale.
- Desi complained that there was **substantially** more homework in her geometry class than there had been last year in her algebra class.

tactic: strategy, plan or scheme for reaching a goal

- Molly's **tactic** for getting her own way was to sit in the corner and pout until someone gave her what she wanted.
- The sergeant had to devise a **tactic** for getting his troops into the country without being seen.

facetious: playful or humorous; joking

- Mike was only being **facetious** when he told Kyle to go jump in the lake.
- Everyone knew Yolanda's remark was **facetious**, so they didn't take offense.

Bonus Words

★misnomer: a wrong or inaccurate name for something

- "The name 'Sunny' is a **misnomer** for that girl. She is the grumpiest person I know," said Dean.
- "'The Good Eat Diner' is definitely a **misnomer**," said Samantha. "After eating at that crummy restaurant last night, I still feel sick!"

★skulk: to slink or move in a slinking way

- Eli **skulked** into the kitchen in the middle of the night and stole a bag of potato chips.
- You could tell Richard was the villain in the school play by the way he **skulked** onto stage.

Name ______________________

Test

Matching

Match each word in the left column to its correct definition in the right column.

____ 1. equitable
____ 2. tactic
____ 3. facetious
____ 4. coagulate
____ 5. belligerent
____ 6. infallible
____ 7. substantial
____ 8. acronym
____ 9. obsolete
____ 10. candid

★Bonus Words

____ 11. skulk
____ 12. misnomer

a. no longer in use or in fashion
b. to clot
c. to cling
d. to sing
e. to slink or move in a slinking way
f. showing a readiness to argue or quarrel
g. playful or humorous; joking
h. incapable of error; never wrong
i. open and honest
j. fair to all concerned
k. a word formed from the first letters of several other words
l. considerable; large; significant
m. pretending not to know a brother or sister who is doing something embarrassing
n. strategy, plan or scheme for reaching a goal
o. a wrong or inaccurate name for something

Fill-in-the-Blank

Directions: The first 10 words listed above belong in the story below. Read the story and use the clues in the text to place each word in the correct blank space provided. You may change the form of a word to fit the story, if you need to. (For example, you might need to add *ed, ing, ly* or *s.*)

Mystery in the O.R.

"How is he, Doctor Herbert? How's my husband? Is he going to live?" asked Mrs. Bertinelli.

Dr. Herbert was known for being (1)________________. "Ms. Bertinelli, the toothbrush in your husband's stomach poses a pretty (2)________________ danger. If we don't remove it soon, he may die."

"Do whatever you need to do, whatever it takes. I trust you completely."

"Mrs. Bertinelli, I just want you to prepare yourself. Mistakes happen, and I make them as much as anybody. After all, I'm not (3)________________." One of the doctor's (4)________________ for helping families trust him was to admit that he wasn't perfect.

On his way to the operating room, Dr. Herbert reviewed the planned surgery with the young medical student who would be observing the operation. "We'll make a two-inch incision in the upper abdomen and then go in with the salad tongs."

The student looked alarmed. "Salad tongs, Doctor? Isn't that a little . . ."

"Lighten up there, Big Guy, I'm just being (5)________________. You don't think I'd really use kitchen utensils in the O.R., do you?"

Dr. Herbert loved saying "O.R." because he loved (6)________________. He used them all the time. He had almost signed on as a team doctor for the Denver Broncos just because he liked saying "N.F.L."

Once in surgery, Dr. Herbert complained, as usual, about the medical equipment. "What is it with this hospital? When did they buy this scalpel, anyway? 1952? How can they expect me to work with this (7)________________ equipment? St. Luke's hospital has *great* equipment. It's certainly not (8)________________ for one hospital to have everything and another to have nothing. Martin, did you tell them I want new equipment? If you didn't, you're fired."

Nurse Martin didn't pay attention to Dr. Herbert's threats. Dr. Herbert always got a bit (9)________________ when he was in the middle of a difficult surgery. He returned to his gentle nature immediately afterwards.

Finally, Dr. Herbert pulled out the toothbrush and held it in the air as though it were a trophy. "I did it!" he shouted. "Once again, I have saved a life with this shoddy equipment."

After Dr. Herbert made sure the patient's blood (10)________________ normally, so that there was no risk of his bleeding to death, he went looking for Mrs. Bertinelli.

"He's going to be fine," he said. "Now I'll ask the question I've been dying to ask from the beginning. *How* did your husband get a toothbrush in his stomach?"

Mrs. Bertinelli looked at Dr. Herbert out of the corner of her eye and shrugged her shoulders mysteriously. That was all the answer he would get from her for now.

Super Challenge

Directions: Use the bonus words from the test to finish the story above.

Vocabulary List #23

abyss: a bottomless pit; something immeasurably deep

- Putting something in Christopher's locker is like throwing it into an **abyss**. He'll never find it.
- The submarine sank into the **abyss** and was never seen again.

fluke: luck; chance

- When Alexis hit the bull's eye the very first time she played darts, everyone said it was just a **fluke**.
- Everyone thought it was a **fluke** when Salvador won the race. They didn't know he had been training for over a year.

plausible: appearing reasonable or possible

- "You didn't finish your homework because your arm froze up last night when it snowed? I'm sorry Richard, but that's just not a **plausible** excuse," said Mrs. Elroy.
- Libby was relieved when the excuse seemed **plausible** to her swimming teacher, but she vowed never to lie again.

itinerary: a detailed plan for a journey

- The **itinerary** for our vacation was so full that we never got to slow down and relax.
- The travel agency usually includes an **itinerary** with a person's plane tickets.

picturesque: beautiful and scenic

- With a clear running stream, beautiful wildflowers and deer grazing in the grass, the valley was truly **picturesque**.
- The countryside in England is **picturesque**, especially in the springtime when the trees and flowers bloom.

frivolous: silly; impractical

- Sondra spent her allowance on **frivolous** things like bubble gum and glittery gold nail polish.
- Kyla spent her time studying for the college entrance exams. Twyla spent her time on more **frivolous** things like cruising the mall and sun bathing.

perjure: to lie while under oath

- You can get in a lot of trouble if you **perjure** yourself. It's best to tell the truth.
- To protect his friend from going to jail with him, the thief **perjured** himself in court and said he was alone the night of the burglary.

balderdash: nonsense

- If something sounds too good to be true, it probably *is* too good to be true. It is **balderdash** to think that you can save a thousand dollars just by changing phone companies.
- "That's **balderdash**!" cried the mayor when his opponent accused him of fraud.

ingenuity: cleverness; imagination

- Audrey showed incredible **ingenuity** by making a costume out of nothing but black plastic trash bags.
- One thing the winners of the science fair had in common was their **ingenuity**.

accentuate: to emphasize

- The model used dark red blusher to **accentuate** her cheekbones.
- Lorraine shouldn't wear green because it just **accentuates** her sickly green complexion.

Bonus Words

★epitome: someone or something that shows all the typical qualities of a group or class

- Some people thought Elwood was the **epitome** of success. Others thought he was just a conceited, arrogant fake.
- Francie thought her father's girlfriend was the **epitome** of evil, but her dad thought she was pretty nice.

★affluent: wealthy

- When Lucinda saw the huge yards, fountains and six-car garages, she knew the neighborhood was **affluent**.
- One of Izzie's grandmas lives in a tiny studio apartment. The other lives in a fancy mansion in an **affluent** part of town.

Name ____________________________

Test

Matching

Match each word in the left column to its correct definition in the right column.

____ 1. frivolous
____ 2. picturesque
____ 3. itinerary
____ 4. ingenuity
____ 5. accentuate
____ 6. abyss
____ 7. plausible
____ 8. fluke
____ 9. balderdash
____ 10. perjure

★Bonus Words

____ 11. epitome
____ 12. affluent

a. nonsense
b. cleverness; imagination
c. wealthy
d. extremely stubborn; immovable
e. someone or something that shows all the typical qualities of a group or class
f. a musical instrument popular in orchestras
g a bottomless pit; something immeasurably deep
h. luck; chance
i. to emphasize
j. miniature paintings
k. appearing reasonable or possible
l. a detailed plan for a journey
m. beautiful and scenic
n. silly; impractical
o. to lie while under oath

Fill-in-the-Blank

Directions: The first 10 words listed above belong in the story below. Read the story and use the clues in the text to place each word in the correct blank space provided. You may change the form of a word to fit the story, if you need to. (For example, you might need to add *ed, ing, ly* or *s.)*

A Kitchen Fit for a Star

It was just a (1)________________ that Lyle got to fly to Hollywood and design a window for the movie star Natalie Youngblood's kitchen. His name had been drawn from a hat filled with the names of all the other Geller Glass employees. But when he arrived at

Natalie's posh home, he informed the star that he had been specifically chosen for the job because of his (2)__________________ with glass.

Lyle was typically an honest man. In just a few minutes, his lie bothered him. "Ms. Youngblood, if I'd been in a courtroom this morning, I would have (3)_______________ myself. I was speaking (4)_______________ a few minutes ago when I said my skill and imagination got me here. My name was drawn from a hat. I guess the long plane ride has affected my mind."

Finding Lyle's excuse for his lie quite (5)_______________, the movie star led him through a dark kitchen to the back yard. The view took Lyle's breath away. It was so (6)_________________. A small stream bubbled between two hills lined with tiny trees. If his (7)________________ for the trip hadn't been so full, Lyle would have stayed on the patio for seven days straight, gazing at the landscape. As it was, he had to finish this job and then fly to three other cities.

Lyle at first thought it was a (8)_________________ expense for Natalie to fly him all the way out here. She could have saved a lot of money just sending him the dimensions and letting him design the window back home. Now that he was here, though, he understood why she had wanted him to see the view first. It was beautiful.

"As you have probably guessed," Natalie crooned, "I don't spend a lot of time in the kitchen. But GBS is doing a special next month called 'Cooking with the Stars.' I'm the first star they're cooking with— unless you count Jessica O'Neil, who would hardly be considered a star at all if she hadn't gotten lucky and won that one Academy Award. Anyway, I don't want them saying my kitchen is just a huge, dark (9)_______________ that happens to have an oven and refrigerator in it. A large window with a view of this landscape would certainly brighten it up a bit, don't you think?"

Having read in *Star Magazine* that Natalie was a notoriously bad cook, Lyle couldn't help but ask what she planned to cook for the show.

"I'm thinking maybe a blueberry pie. My eyes are hazel, and the blue would (10)________________ them quite nicely. Don't you agree? If this window turns out well, I'll have someone put in a sparkling blue lake right where you're standing."

Super Challenge

Directions: Use the bonus words from the test to finish the story above.

Vocabulary List #24

culmination: the high point

- For Susan, the **culmination** of the weekend's festivities was when her favorite poet read her favorite poem.
- The **culmination** of Hannah's birthday party was when she got to blow out the candles on her cake.

ominous: threatening

- There was something **ominous** about the man's face and movements. The couple decided to get away from him, fast.
- The dark, rolling clouds were **ominous**, so the picnickers packed up and went home.

diminutive: tiny

- The Chihuahua is a **diminutive** breed of dog. You could probably fit one in your pocket.
- La Donna's cat was **diminutive**, especially when compared to Val's cat, who weighed nearly 20 pounds.

perpetual: going on forever

- The town seemed to be experiencing a **perpetual** winter. The snow kept falling and falling, even though it was summer.
- "Candace's **perpetual** complaining leaves me tired and wanting to pull my hair out," said her mother.

terse: brief; to the point

- Corey was a coward. Instead of breaking up with Hillary face to face, he wrote her a **terse** letter.
- When Samuel asked why he was being sent to the principal's office, Mr. Walker gave only a **terse** reply.

purge: to get rid of something undesirable

- The club officers **purged** the secret club of members who might betray the organization.
- Before he skipped town, the crooked accountant **purged** his files of any evidence that he had been embezzling.

panorama: a full view of an area

- The **panorama** from the Empire State building is breathtaking.
- After reaching the summit of Pike's Peak, Jody had a **panoramic** view of the whole area.

gregarious: sociable; fond of the company of others

- Madison was elected captain because her **gregarious** nature made her so popular.
- Karlie was so **gregarious** she never missed a chance to attend a party.

rebuttal: a "return" argument to something just said

- "Your **rebuttal** is full of holes and lies," said the prosecutor to the defense team.
- When a group of adults wrote a letter to the newspaper complaining about MTV, a group of teens wrote a **rebuttal** listing the good things about the channel.

effervescent: bubbly; lively

- After Heath shook up the can of Coke and opened it, the **effervescent** liquid spilled all over the desk.
- Bethany will be a perfect beauty pageant contestant because she is so **effervescent**.

Bonus Words

★emulate: to strive to equal or surpass

- James practiced his violin everyday, trying to **emulate** his uncle who played with a symphony orchestra.
- Rex's dad would like it better if Rex tried to **emulate** Albert Einstein or Isaac Newton instead of Sylvester Stallone.

★vacillate: to go back and forth

- Her biggest fault was that she couldn't seem to make a decision. She could **vacillate** forever.
- Elmer **vacillated** between asking Cassie and asking Pauline to the dance.

Name ______________________________

Test

Matching

Match each word in the left column to its correct definition in the right column.

____ 1. purge
____ 2. panorama
____ 3. perpetual
____ 4. rebuttal
____ 5. effervescent
____ 6. ominous
____ 7. diminutive
____ 8. gregarious
____ 9. terse
____ 10. culmination

★Bonus Words

____ 11. emulate
____ 12. vacillate

a. a "return" argument to something just said
b. threatening
c. tiny
d. sociable; fond of the company of others
e. to go back and forth
f. to sit
g. to stay
h. to roll over
i. brief; to the point
j. to get rid of something undesirable
k. to strive to equal or surpass
l. the high point
m. a full view of an area
n. going on forever
o. bubbly; lively

Fill-in-the-Blank

Directions: The first 10 words listed above belong in the story below. Read the story and use the clues in the text to place each word in the correct blank space provided. You may change the form of a word to fit the story, if you need to. (For example, you might need to add *ed, ing, ly* or *s*.)

Lazy Prince Dudley and the Dragon

Prince Dudley yawned. His father the king had been ranting and raving about the kingdom's fire-breathing-dragon problem for over an hour. The old king was a (1)_______________ fellow who would rather throw a feast for his friends than fight a dragon. But he was a dutiful king, and had been trying to (2)_______________ his kingdom of evil dragons his whole life. He never could seem to get rid of the horrible things completely. Just when he thought he had run them all out, he would see an (3)________________ cloud of smoke on the horizon. When he rode his horse in that direction, he inevitably found yet another village burned to the ground by the fiery breath of yet another dragon. He was too old for this. "Why haven't exterminators been invented yet?" he raved. Finally, the king paused, adding, "Get on that expensive horse I bought you and go fight a dragon for once, Dudley." He frowned. "Go," he said (4)________________. Prince Dudley wasn't used to his father being so brief with him.

Prince Dudley, who wasn't exactly (5)________________ with excitement, yawned again. "What a bore to go fight dragons. And yet, beating this particular dragon could be the (6)________________of my princely young career. It might bring me great respect and devotion from the people."

With a great display of bravery, the prince walked grandly out of the castle, swishing his cape for effect. Pleased with his performance, the prince was sorry that the only horse he had to jump onto was such a (7)________________ one. (The expensive horse he'd gotten for his birthday had long since run off to find a more exciting owner.) Dudley rode off with his feet dragging on the ground.

He scanned the (8)________________ as he rode until he saw the cave of the dragon. Not wanting to confront the dragon, he wrote the words "Drop dead!" on a piece of paper, tied the paper to a rock and threw it into the cave. Then he hid behind some trees a safe distance away.

The dragon opened the note and tried to read it. Just as he remembered he didn't know how to read, he saw Prince Dudley's hiding place and drew in a huge breath. Then he released an explosion of flames in Prince Dudley's direction. "Go away!" the dragon warned between sparks.

Emerging from behind charred trees Prince Dudley did not have a (9)________________ for what the dragon had just said. With knees knocking together, he mounted his short horse and took off at top speed toward home.

The king would simply have to realize that there was nothing to do about the (10)__________________ problem of dragons. "It obviously will never go away," the prince told his father between yawns. "I did all I could to eliminate the wretched beast."

Super Challenge

Directions: Use the bonus words from the test to finish the story above.

	1	2	3	4	5	6	7	8
V	misnomer	benevolent	gregarious	coincidental	tintinnabulation★	facetious	effervescent	ruminate
O	accentuate	shoat ★	plausible	intaglio ★	affluent	qualms	wentletrap ★	perjure
C	picturesque	infallible	stringent	fluke	tactic	perpetual	belligerent	frivolous
A	gaberlunzie ★	coalition	purge	epitome	diminutive	skulk	ambrosia	bubo ★
B	acronym	rebuttal	coagulate	quisling ★	futile	emulate	terse	equitable
R	incensed	abyss	panorama	obsolete	vacillate	substantial	ludicrous	culmination
A	ominous	abolish	ingenuity	vicariously	candid	peccadillo ★	itinerary	balderdash

Appendix

Alphabetical List of All Words in Abra Vocabra

Regular Words

abduct
abhor
abolish
abundant
abyss
accentuate
acquitted
acronym
aghast
amble
ambrosia
anecdote
anguish
annual
apprehend
atheist
authentic
balderdash
barbaric
belligerent
benevolent
bicker
blunder
bogus
boisterous
bravado
brutal
candid
candor
cantankerous
careen
chaos
charisma
cliché
coagulate
coalition
coddle
coincidental
compassion
comprehend
concise
concur
condone
consequence
console
contempt
controversial
convene
cordial
corpulent
culmination
dank
dictator
diffuse
dignity
dilapidated
diligent
diminutive
dismembered
dupe
ebony
eccentric
ecstatic
effervescent
egotistical
emerge
engrossed
equitable
erroneous
eternal
ethical
excerpt
expectorate
extrovert
facetious
facsimile
feline
fiasco
fickle
flourish
fluent
fluke
fortnight
fragile
frivolous
futile
gaunt
gawk
glutton
gregarious
grimace
grisly
grotesque
guerrilla
guffaw
gullible
habitually
haphazard
hostile
idolize
immortal
imperceptible
inadvertent
inanimate
inaudible
incensed
incompatible
indignant
inebriated
infallible
infatuated
infinite
ingenuity
innovation
insolent
interrogate
interval
intoxicated
intricate
introvert
irate
irrelevant
itinerary
jeer
jovial
kleptomaniac
lackluster
lament
loathe
lucrative
ludicrous
lustrous
malady
maternal
meager
meddle
mediate
melodramatic
memorabilia
minuscule
monotonous
morale
morbid
mortal
mortified
nocturnal
obese
oblivious
obsolete
obstinate
ominous
opaque
optimistic
orb
panorama
paradox

Alphabetical list

paranoid
paunch
peal
perjure
perpetual
perplexed
persnickety
pessimistic
philanthropist
picturesque
plagiarize
plausible
ponder
profit
profound
prominent
prompt
proprietor
prudent
pseudonym
pungent

purge
qualms
quibble
ravenous
rebuttal
reciprocate
recoil
redundant
remorseful
replenish
retrieve
sallow
sarcastic
secluded
seethe
sentimental
shun
significant
simultaneously
sinister
smitten

smug
somber
soothe
squalor
stringent
submerge
subsequent
substantial
succinct
sulk
swagger
synopsis
taboo
tactic
tangible
terrain
terrorism
terse
textiles
tout
toxic

tragic
tranquil
transition
turbulent
tyrant
unscrupulous
vain
valiant
vast
venomous
verbatim
verify
vermin
versatile
veto
vice
virtue
virtuoso
vivacious
vivid
wrath

Bonus Words

a cappella
affluent
albatross
altruistic
ambiguous
amend
astute
avaricious
befuddle
capitulate
carcinogenic
chastise

compelling
consensus
countenance
despondent
destitute
dumbfounded
emulate
epitome
extemporaneous
façade
faux
filibuster

gargantuan
genial
gobbledygook
grovel
gumption
hoodwink
impeccable
innate
intermittent
mesmerize
misnomer
omen

omnipotent
palatial
placate
precocious
ruminate
skulk
translucent
vacillate
vehement
vicariously
vindictive
waiver

Word Lists at a Glance

Word List 1
annual
grotesque
gawk
obese
toxic
blunder
bicker
brutal
feline
tyrant

Bonus Words
dumbfounded
waiver

Word List 2
fragile
vast
swagger
vivid
soothe
glutton
irate
prompt
dictator
intoxicated

Bonus Words
palatial
omen

Word List 3
immortal
pessimistic
barbaric
tragic
sulk
compassion
mortal
recoil
optimistic
vain

Bonus Words
gargantuan
hoodwink

Word List 4
fluent
console
memorabilia
expectorate
amble
meager
maternal
guffaw
egotistical
monotonous

Bonus Words
avaricious
gumption

Word List 5
intricate
dank
lackluster
inaudible
dismember
submerge
lustrous
inebriated
ponder
authentic

Bonus Words
compel
genial

Word List 6
jovial
careen
minuscule
squalor
morbid
pseudonym
grimace
wrath
tranquil
sallow

Bonus Words
intermittent
a cappella

Word List 7
cordial
acquitted
virtue
significant
dignity
melodramatic
eternal
paranoid
emerge
chaos

Bonus Words
impeccable
grovel

Word List 8
hostile
anguish
boisterous
interrogate
bogus
charisma
dilapidated
ecstatic
sinister
philanthropist

Bonus Words
ambiguous
befuddle

Word List 9
infatuated
habitually
ebony
mortified
plagiarize
remorseful
venomous
opaque
guerrilla
succinct

Bonus Words
vindictive
amend

Word List 10
taboo
persnickety
haphazard
imperceptible
atheist
shun
anecdote
concur
vivacious
perplexed

Bonus Words
capitulate
consensus

Word List 11
infinite
abduct
textiles
loathe
unscrupulous
controversial
turbulent
nocturnal
tout
smug

Bonus Words
façade
vehement

Word List 12
aghast
redundant
gullible
eccentric
inanimate
jeer
ravenous
valiant
paradox
flourish

Bonus Words
mesmerize
destitute

Word List 13
synopsis
idolize
inadvertent
verify
convene
excerpt
lucrative
orb
lament
candor

Bonus Words
faux
precocious

Word List 14
seethe
incompatible
paunch
proprietor
vermin
fickle
smitten
gaunt
meddle
kleptomaniac

Bonus Words
astute
filibuster

Word List 15
veto
prominent
ethical
cliché
introvert
extrovert
comprehend
profound
transition
simultaneously

Bonus Words
gobbledygook
carcinogenic

Word List 16
indignant
pungent
grisly
consequence
versatile
abundant
somber
erroneous
secluded
fiasco

Bonus Words
translucent
placate

Word List 17
morale
sarcastic
vice
contempt
oblivious
apprehend
terrain
diligent
virtuoso
prudent

Bonus Words
extemporaneous
altruistic

Words List 18
subsequent
facsimile
retrieve
engrossed
concise
fortnight
mediate
corpulent
bravado
terrorism

Bonus Words
despondent
albatross

Word List 19
quibble
malady
condone
sentimental
obstinate
tangible
profit
innovation
replenish
irrelevant

Bonus Words
chastise
countenance

Word List 20
dupe
cantankerous
insolent
coddle
reciprocate
verbatim
diffuse
peal
interval
abhor

Bonus Words
innate
omnipotent

Word List 21
stringent
qualms
incensed
benevolent
futile
ludicrous
ambrosia
coincidental
abolish
coalition

Bonus Words
vicariously
ruminate

Word List 22
coagulate
equitable
obsolete
belligerent
candid
infallible
acronym
substantial
tactic
facetious

Bonus Words
misnomer
skulk

Word List 23
abyss
fluke
plausible
itinerary
picturesque
frivolous
perjure
balderdash
ingenuity
accentuate

Bonus Words
epitome
affluent

Word List 24
culmination
ominous
diminutive
gregarious
terse
purge
panorama
perpetual
rebuttal
effervescent

Bonus Words
emulate
vacillate

Pieces for Vocabra Game

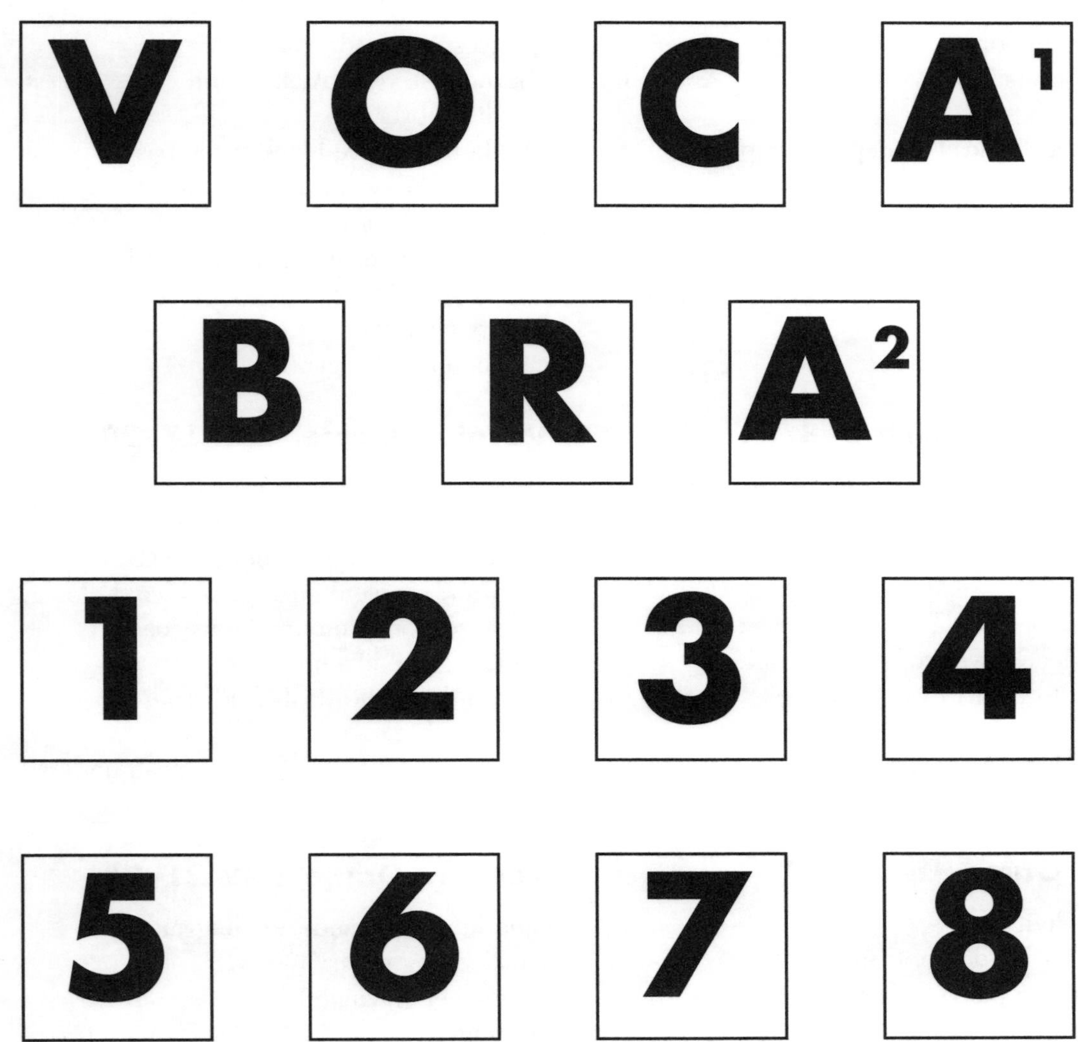

Definitions of Weird Words

Vocabra Game, Lists 1–4

picayune: unimportant, petty
burnoose: a long hooded cloak worn by Arabs and Moors
mugwump: a politically independent person
flibbertigibbet: an irresponsible, flighty person
hegira: a journey of escape
jacktar: sailor
ghee: clarified butter from the butterfat of buffalo or other milk
inveigle: to win by flattery

Vocabra Game, Lists 5–8

ylangylang: oil or perfume from the Asian ylangylang tree
zebu: ox-like animal from Africa
hawser: large rope
vichyssoise: potato soup, usually served cold
gewgaw: a decorative trinket or bauble
peplum: a short skirt or ruffle attached at the waistline
lederhosen: leather shorts
katydid: tree insect resembling a grasshopper

Vocabra Game, Lists 9–12

filbert: hazelnut
hotspur: a hot-headed person
plectrum: a thin piece of metal to pluck the strings of a stringed instrument
zither: a stringed musical instrument
poltroon: a complete coward
howdah: seat for riding on an elephant
gravid: pregnant
squamulose: scaly

Vocabra Game, Lists 13–16

galluses: suspenders
chernozem: very black topsoil
pugilist: boxer
plinth: the square block at the base of a column, pedestal or statue
jape: to tease or jest
spoonerism: changing around the initial sounds of words (big jerk = jig berk)
knout: a whip
catamount: a cougar

Vocabra Game, Lists 17–20

scimitar: short, curved sword
xenophobia: fear of strangers
rococo: elaborate style of architecture
williwaw: a violent gust of cold wind blowing seaward from a mountainous coast
quoit: a game like horseshoes
yegg: a thief who steals from safes
curlew: a bird
tsunami: a giant wave caused by an undersea earthquake

Vocabra Game, Lists 21–24

gaberlunzie: a wandering beggar
shoat: young pig (swine)
intaglio: engraving in stone
quisling: a traitor
tintinnabulation: the ringing of bells
peccadillo: a minor or petty sin
wentletrap: a kind of marine snail
bubo: an inflamed swelling

Test Answer Keys

Note: Answers will vary for the "Super Challenge" portion of each test. The examples below are included to show possibilities.

List #1, Answer Key

Matching

1. g
2. j
3. l
4. a
5. k
6. d
7. i
8. b
9. f
10. h

Bonus words

11. e
12. n

Fill-in-the-Blank

1. gawked
2. obese
3. feline
4. grotesque
5. blunders
6. tyrant
7. bickering
8. toxic
9. annual
10. brutal

Super Challenge

When Jason woke up the next morning, he rode his bike straight to the animal shelter to get himself an attack cat to protect him from Scott. But when he walked into the room full of cages with howling animals, the first thing he saw was a cage full of tiny puppies, whimpering quietly. Jason was **dumbfounded**. He wanted to speak but he couldn't. The little things were so sweet. "I'll take that one," he finally blurted out.

"Okay, but first you have to get your parents' permission," said the woman who showed Jason into the kennel.

When Jason called his mom and asked her permission, she made him promise to take care of the animal himself. "You're going to have to come home and walk your dog. I should make you sign a **waiver** giving up your rights to go to your friend's house after school every day."

"I promise I'll take care of it," Jason said.

"By the way, what kind of dog is it?" his mother asked.

"Well, the lady here said it's a mutt. But it looks like a Scottie to me."

List #2, Answer Key

Matching

1. n
2. g
3. k
4. f
5. m
6. l
7. j
8. d
9. b
10. a

Bonus words

11. e
12. i

Fill-in-the-Blank

1. irate
2. vast
3. soothe
4. glutton
5. dictator
6. swaggers
7. intoxicated
8. promptly
9. fragile
10. vivid

Super Challenge

Wanda felt so good after standing up to her boss that she rode the city bus all the way across town to visit her Aunt Selma. Besides being her favorite aunt, Selma was also Wanda's rich aunt. She lived in a **palatial** estate with 23 servants.

After the butler led Wanda to her aunt's sun room, Aunt Selma's face lit up. "Your arrival is such a good **omen**," she cried. "I know I'll be able to finish my project now. In fact, I'll hire you to help!"

List #3, Answer Key

Matching
1. h
2. c
3. a
4. b
5. d
6. m
7. f
8. i
9. l
10. j

Bonus words
11. n
12. e

Fill-in-the-Blank
1. barbaric
2. immortal
3. vain
4. mortal
5. pessimistic
6. tragic
7. recoiled
8. sulked
9. compassion
10. optimistic

Super Challenge

Miranda was annoyed and had a **gargantuan** case of jealousy. She had never seen a troll as handsome as Sebastian. She decided to try to **hoodwink** him into leaving Yolanda for her.

"I am really a beautiful, rich princess who has been turned into a troll," she said. "To share all my riches, all you need to do is marry me. Then I'll become beautiful again."

Sebastian was smart as well as handsome. He didn't marry her.

List #4, Answer Key

Matching
1. g
2. h
3. f
4. n
5. i
6. c
7. k
8. l
9. a
10. b

Bonus words
11. o
12. d

Fill-in-the-Blank
1. maternal
2. expectorate
3. console
4. fluent
5. ambled
6. guffaw
7. meager
8. memorabilia
9. egotistical
10. monotonous

Super Challenge

It was an entire month before Antonio got the **gumption** to ask Uncle Lou what happened to all his furniture.

"After I quit playing baseball," Uncle Lou said, "I had a hard time paying my rent, so my landlord took the sofa as payment. Well, my furniture was so nice, and the **avaricious** old man liked it so much that he raised my rent. The next month, I had to give him my love seat and an easy chair. Then it was the end tables. When he started eyeing my bedroom dresser, I decided to get out of there. I moved to this apartment, and that's when I realized I kind of liked having a lot of space . . . Hey, did I ever tell you my batting average?"

List #5, Answer Key

Matching
1. d
2. j
3. n
4. a
5. c
6. f
7. i
8. o
9. k
10. l

Bonus Words

11. h
12. e

Fill-in-the-Blank
1. submerged
2. dismembered
3. pondering
4. inebriated
5. lustrous
6. intricate
7. dank
8. inaudible
9. lackluster
10. authentic

Super Challenge

"From the look on your faces, I take it you didn't get a real **genial** reception down in that ship," Hank remarked.

"There's a ghost down there," said Carmine as he shuddered.

"You don't say," answered Hank. He started to row the boat toward shore. Since he had them in the boat, Hank knew he was **compelled** to listen to their story —one he had heard many times before. When Red Eye Malone signaled from a nearby boat, Hank smiled. Once more, he and Red Eye had scared off curious explorers who might discover where they kept their supply of stolen whisky and rum.

List #6, Answer Key

Matching
1. f
2. a
3. l
4. e
5. i
6. o
7. j
8. k
9. m
10. n

Bonus Words

11. c
12. b

Fill-in-the-Blank
1. tranquil
2. jovial
3. pseudonym
4. minuscule
5. squalor
6. sallow
7. morbid
8. grimaced
9. wrath
10. careen

Super Challenge

"So he never comes out of his house anymore?" I asked.

"Not very often. I do see him every Tuesday evening when he goes to the church over in Joeville, where his sister lives," Grandpa Sam answered.

"He sings in the **a cappella** choir over there. It's a poor congregation and they can't afford to buy an organ. His sister Maisie Raisin, tells me that Old Man Ventana doesn't ever sing a song all the way through. He just sings **intermittently** because every time the choir sings the word 'praise' he gets angry because 'praise' sounds like 'raisin.' The same thing happens when they sing 'risen.' And you know those are pretty common words in church singing."

List #7, Answer Key

Matching
1. c
2. k
3. o
4. d
5. g
6. a
7. j
8. f
9. e
10. b

Bonus Words
11. i
12. n

Fill-in-the-Blank
1. chaos
2. emerged
3. significant
4. cordial
5. paranoid
6. virtue
7. eternally
8. melodramatic
9. dignity
10. acquitted

Super Challenge
Before she left the courthouse, Miss Muffet ducked into the restroom. She added more lip gloss and blush to get that **impeccable** appearance she was so famous for. She wanted to make the most of the publicity she was getting. She also wanted to look great for Georgie. She was sure he was interested in her.

When she stepped out of the restroom, Georgie scowled at her. "I'm through with you, Miss Muffet," he said.

"Why?" Miss Muffet gasped.

"You looked ridiculous when you **groveled** back in the courtroom. I'm glad we won the trial, but your behavior was horrible. I could never trust anyone who acts like that," Georgie answered.

"Well, I never," Miss Muffet said, disgusted. She put on her little red riding hood and stomped off to meet her public. She thought to herself "Who needs that little weasel anyway?"

List #8, Answer Key

Matching
1. l
2. i
3. a
4. e
5. h
6. k
7. g
8. b
9. c
10. m

Bonus Words
11. f
12. j

Fill-in-the-Blank
1. ecstatic
2. dilapidated
3. sinister
4. anguish
5. philanthropist
6. hostile
7. interrogate
8. boisterous
9. bogus
10. charisma

Super Challenge
Gazbot looked down at the Intruder badge and wondered, "What does 'intruder' mean?" She remembered that the word was sometimes used to refer to someone who broke into houses to steal things. Gazbot didn't think that Fran was there to steal anything.

"I guess this is just another **ambiguous** earthling word," she thought.

There were so many words and so many behaviors that she didn't understand. She spent most of her time on earth **befuddled**. She couldn't wait to get back to Mars, where things were clearer. Also, on Mars, it was easier being green.

List #9, Answer Key

Matching
1. a
2. n
3. i
4. g
5. d
6. j
7. b
8. o
9. e
10. h

Bonus Words
11. m
12. l

Fill-in-the-Blank
1. infatuated
2. ebony
3. guerrilla
4. opaque
5. habitual
6. mortified
7. plagiarize
8. remorseful
9. venomous
10. succinct

Super Challenge

Mrs. Goldberg had had enough. "All right, Mister, it's detention for you. I'll see you here after school." Elvis could take it no longer.

"Mrs. Goldberg, you're just jealous because you aren't beautiful like Lydia — you're old and wrinkled and . . . and . . ." Elvis stopped, and realized his **vindictive** remarks had hurt Mrs. Goldberg's feelings. "I'm sorry, Mrs. Goldberg. I'll see you after school," he said.

That afternoon, as Elvis sat in detention, the door opened. He looked up and saw the face of a true angel. She floated past his desk, her blond hair flowing behind her, her smile radiating throughout the room. Wow! thought Elvis. I'm going to have to **amend** my thinking about Lydia. Samantha is the girl for me!

List #10, Answer Key

Matching
1. e
2. l
3. m
4. g
5. j
6. b
7. k
8. d
9. f
10. h

Bonus Words
11. o
12. a

Fill-in-the-Blank
1. perplexed
2. persnickety
3. imperceptible
4. concurred
5. haphazard
6. vivacious
7. anecdotes
8. shunned
9. atheist
10. taboo

Super Challenge

The next day Uba again asked both Og and their neighbor about the wooly mammoth tusks. The **consensus** was that they should stay . . . at least until Uba changed her mind again. Then Uba had another question.

"Og," she said, "I think the one thing we are lacking around this house is a pet. I was down at the Tar Pit Fashion Mall, and they had an adorable saber-toothed tiger cub. Wouldn't it be great to have one?"

Og groaned. The last thing he wanted was a saber-toothed tiger to clean up after. "Oh, Uba, I don't know . . . they shed so badly, and where will we put the litter box?"

Uba burst into tears. "You never let me have the things I really want! I don't think you really love me!" Og hated it when Uba cried, so finally he **capitulated**.

"Okay, okay, let's go get the saber-toothed tiger cub. But he's not sleeping on the slab. He has to sleep on the floor."

"Okay, Og, we'll see . . ." Uba said, already trying to figure out where the litter box would look best.

List #11, Answer Key

Matching
1. m
2. l
3. c
4. n
5. g
6. h
7. i
8. d
9. f
10. a

Bonus Words
11. o
12. b

Fill-in-the-Blank
1. nocturnal
2. touted
3. controversial
4. smug
5. infinitely
6. turbulent
7. abduct
8. loathed
9. unscrupulous
10. textile

Super Challenge
In the textile business, maybe people wouldn't get so **vehement** when someone made a tiny little mistake.

Gus felt sad and discouraged, but he put on a happy **façade** and smiled at friends passing by. Super heroes always make the best of things.

List #12, Answer Key

Matching
1. b
2. d
3. n
4. k
5. l
6 m
7. a
8. j
9. o
10. e

Bonus Words
11. g
12. h

Fill-in-the-Blank
1. ravenous
2. aghast
3. eccentric
4. valiantly
5. gullible
6. redundant
7. jeered
8. paradox
9. inanimate
10. flourish

Super Challenge
Ray walked up to Lucinda Gilroy, who was listening to Chuck Feldspar. She was **mesmerized** by Chuck's handsome face and didn't notice Ray, even when he started tossing pieces of popcorn at her.

Feeling disappointed that he couldn't get any attention, Ray sat down by himself and starting eating his popcorn. He hated popcorn. "What a stupid party," he said to himself. "Can't they serve anything better than this? I don't care if they don't have much money. I don't even care if they are **destitute**. They should find the money to serve better snacks than this."

List #13, Answer Key

Matching
1. a
2. n
3. o
4. c
5. f
6. h
7. k
8. j
9. m
10. g

Bonus words

11. b
12. d

Fill-in-the-Blank
1. idolized
2. lamented
3. convened
4. excerpts
5. synopsis
6. inadvertently
7. orb
8. candor
9. verify
10. lucrative

Super Challenge

Thad's mother wasn't finished yet. She was hopping mad and wanted her son's money back.

"Oh no," said Francesca. "This is a strictly cash business. No refunds." Her **faux** pearl earrings jingled as she shook her head. She refused to give the boy a refund.

Just then a little girl came out from behind the curtain. She was only about five years old, but she spoke like a grown-up. "Mother, it is not good business practice to upset the customers. If you don't give this woman her money back, she'll tell everyone in town that you are a crook. But if you do give her the money back, she'll tell people that you are a fair and honest fortune-teller."

Francesca knew her **precocious** little daughter was right. Thad barely noticed as Francesca counted out his money. He was too busy staring at Cali with a goofy grin on his face.

Cali knew that her money had been well-spent.

List #14, Answer Key

Matching
1. k
2. o
3. a
4. c
5. e
6. f
7. g
8. l
9. n
10. d

Bonus Words

11. h
12. j

Fill-in-the-Blank
1. proprietor
2. fickle
3. paunch
4. vermin
5. seethed
6. gaunt
7. smitten
8. incompatible
9. kleptomaniac
10. meddle

Super Challenge

Jim soon decided that the exercise bike was the best machine for him. He didn't get bored because he could watch television while he peddled. He especially liked to watch SNN, the Senate Network News. Whenever a **filibuster** prevented a vote on a bill that he liked, he would get so angry that he would push himself harder and harder and have a great workout.

Jim thought he was an **astute** observer of the political scene. "I can always figure out just how a senator is going to vote," he thought to himself. He was almost always right.

List #15, Answer Key

Matching

1. h
2. e
3. k
4. a
5. j
6. n
7. c
8. f
9. d
10. l

Bonus words

11. i
12. m

Fill-in-the-Blank

1. simultaneously
2. cliché
3. transition
4. introverts
5. extroverts
6. prominent
7. profound
8. comprehend
9. vetoed
10. ethical

Super Challenge

Suddenly there was an explosion outside. Smoke poured into the building.

"Oh dear," worried the principal. "What if these fumes are **carcinogenic**? This meeting is dismissed!"

Mr. Davidson smiled. "Good!" he thought. "Now we don't have to listen to any more of that **gobbledygook**."

List #16, Answer Key

Matching

1. d
2. k
3. o
4. m
5. b
6. e
7. n
8. h
9. j
10. g

Bonus words

11. a
12. f

Fill-in-the-Blank

1. consequences
2. grisly
3. indignant
4. versatile
5. pungent
6. erroneous
7. fiasco
8. abundant
9. secluded
10. somber

Super Challenge

"Come on you guys," Dirk whined. "You all promised. Somebody has to go into the house with me."

"Well, okay, I'll go," Jeanetta said. She knew she had better **placate** him or he'd never let her forget it.

They walked to the next block while the wind blew furiously and the storm clouds darkened the night. When they got to the haunted house, they stood and stared. It looked really scary at night.

"Yikes, look at the front window," Jeannetta whispered. When Dirk focused on the window, he saw a figure behind the **translucent** curtains. He couldn't see clearly, but what he did see was a seven foot tall man with bushy hair holding a knife in one hand and an ax in the other.

There was no more discussion. Everyone left immediately.

List #17, Answer Key

Matching
1. k
2. n
3. f
4. a
5. i
6. l
7. j
8. g
9. e
10. d

Bonus Words

11. o
12. c

Fill-in-the-Blank
1. virtuoso
2. diligent
3. oblivious
4. terrain
5. vice
6. apprehend
7. prudent
8. sarcastic
9. contempt
10. morale

Super Challenge

One day Rachel and Mozy's favorite aunt came for a visit. While Aunt Marie was talking with Rachel and Mozy, she requested a piano recital from them. "I know it is **extemporaneous**," she said, "but I'll take into account that you haven't had time to prepare."

Rachel went white with despair. "After she hears my piano playing compared to Mozy's, she will be disappointed in me," thought Rachel.

"Go first, Rachel," Mozy said. He looked at her with confidence.

Rachel sat down and began to play. She made mistakes — a lot of mistakes. Then Mozy sat down. Rachel expected to hear his usual beautiful, perfect music. Instead, he hit many, many wrong notes.

Later, Rachel asked Mozy why he hadn't played as well as he could have.

"Well . . . I just didn't feel like playing. I was kind of tired," he said.

Rachel knew Mozy wasn't telling the truth. He had acted in an **altruistic** way, unselfishly playing below his potential so that she would look good in front of their aunt.

List #18, Answer Key

Matching
1. j
2. k
3. h
4. b
5. d
6. n
7. e
8. f
9. a
10. l

Bonus Words

11. o
12. i

Fill-in-the-Blank
1. terrorism
2. bravado
3. corpulent
4. subsequent
5. facsimile
6. engrossed
7. fortnight
8. mediate
9. retrieve
10. concise

Super Challenge

Since he hadn't paid attention in class, the upcoming test was an **albatross** for Max. He had to study several hours each night and had no time for anything else, even his yoga. As a result, he grew **despondent**. One evening as Max sulked around the house, his dad asked what was wrong. All Max could say was that he wished he had paid attention in class.

List #19, Answer Key

Matching

1. b
2. l
3. m
4. f
5. j
6. g
7. c
8. i
9. d
10. n

Bonus Words

11. o
12. h

Fill-in-the-Blank

1. tangible
2. innovation
3. sentimental
4. profit
5. obstinate
6. malady
7. condone
8. quibble
9. irrelevant
10. replenish

Super Challenge

To help pay her tuition, Roger and Nancy's daughter Amber began selling the electric automatic toilet paper unwinder on campus. One day, during a demonstration of the device, a six-year-old boy jumped up from the audience and began pushing buttons on it. Toilet paper flew everywhere, catching in the highest branches of the trees, wafting over the grass on a breeze, even wrapping around stuffy Professor Hewitt's face. The campus looked like a blizzard had blown in and left piles of snow.

Fear replaced the pleasure on the boys **countenance** as he saw his mother's angry face. He did not like to be **chastised**.

Amber, however, was happy to see him get in trouble. She was *not* happy to pick up the mess he had made.

List #20, Answer Key

Matching

1. g
2. m
3. h
4. k
5. j
6. b
7. i
8. n
9. d
10. f

Bonus Words

11. a
12. c

Fill-in-the-Blank

1. cantankerous
2. coddled
3. intervals
4. verbatim
5. peal
6. insolent
7. diffused
8. reciprocate
9. dupe
10. abhorred

Super Challenge

One day a beautiful girl walked into the Tasty Freeze and complimented Travis on the fudge cones and banana splits he made. It was love at first sight. Travis let her compliments go to his head. He felt **omnipotent**, as though he could make the world's best shake – or anything else.

She ordered a hot fudge sundae and asked sweetly if she could pour the chocolate syrup on the ice cream herself. Because Travis was in love with the girl, he let her. She took the bottle and squeezed the chocolate syrup all over Travis' head.

"That's for my little brother Billy," she said .

Travis just stood there, dripping chocolate syrup onto the blue speckled floor. "That family must have an **innate** need to play with chocolate," he said to his co-worker.

List #21, Answer Key

Matching
1. b
2. d
3. l
4. m
5. j
6. e
7. o
8. f
9. i
10. a

Bonus Words
11. n
12. h

Fill-in-the-Blank
1. stringent
2. ambrosia
3. ludicrous
4. incensed
5. futile
6. qualms
7. benevolent
8. coalition
9. abolished
10. coincidental

Super Challenge

A local newspaper finally asked him why he had started the duck rescue program. He said that after the Last Quack Duck Head Pie incident, he had **ruminated** a long time about the plight of ducks in chef schools. After meditating for three weeks, Anthony decided to start the program.

"I didn't want to live **vicariously** through other people who were saving animals," he said. I wanted to live my own life and help animals. Now I am doing it and loving it. I have also made some lovely duck friends whom I will never cook into any of my meals."

List #22, Answer Key

Matching
1. j
2. n
3. g
4. b
5. f
6. h
7. l
8. k
9. a
10. i

Bonus Words
11. e
12. o

Fill-in-the-Blank
1. candid
2. substantial
3. infallible
4. tactics
5. facetious
6. acronyms
7. obsolete
8. equitable
9. belligerent
10. coagulated

Super Challenge

Mrs. Bertinelli wasn't about to tell the doctor about her husband's horrible habit. He **skulked** around the neighborhood alleys at night and ate things from garbage cans. His habit, of course, was both embarrassing and dangerous. She wasn't even going to think about how he managed to swallow a toothbrush instead of someone's leftover corn chips or tuna casserole.

"Your husband is a prince," smiled Dr. Herbert.

"That's a **misnomer** if I ever heard one," she thought. "He's not a prince. He's a bum!"

List #23, Answer Key

Matching

1. n
2. m
3. l
4. b
5. i
6. g
7. k
8. h
9. a
10. o

Bonus Words

11. e
12. c

Fill-in-the-Blank

1. fluke
2. ingenuity
3. perjured
4. balderdash
5. plausible
6. picturesque
7. itinerary
8. frivolous
9. abyss
10. accentuate

Super Challenge

Lyle thought to himself, "She really is the **epitome** of the self-centered, **affluent** movie star. She is so conceited and so rich!"

List #24, Answer Key

Matching

1. j
2. m
3. n
4. a
5. o
6. b
7. c
8. d
9. i
10. l

Bonus Words

11. k
12. e

Fill-in-the-Blank

1. gregarious
2. purge
3. ominous
4. tersely
5. effervescent
6. culmination
7. diminutive
8. panorama
9. rebuttal
10. perpetual

Super Challenge

The king shook his head, disappointed in his son. "You give up so easily," he said. "I wish you would try to **emulate** your Uncle Frank, who would work at a problem until he solved it."

"I know I'm a disappointment to you," said Dudley. "Maybe I should try again . . . Maybe I shouldn't." He **vacillated** between going and not going until his father threw up his hands in despair.

"I'm calling your Uncle Frank," he said.

Other Titles from Cottonwood Press

To Order More Copies of AbraVocabra

Please send me ______ copies of *AbraVocabra*. I am enclosing $21.95, plus shipping and handling ($4.00 for one book, $2.00 for each additional book). Colorado residents add 66¢ sales tax, per book. Total amount $_______.

Name ____

(School) ____
(Include only if using school address.)

Address ____

City ______________________ State ______ Zip Code __________

Method of Payment:

❑Payment enclosed ❑Visa ❑MasterCard ❑Discover ❑Purchase Order

Credit Card# ______________________ Expiration Date __________

Signature ____

Send to:

Cottonwood Press, Inc.
107 Cameron Drive
Fort Collins, CO 80525
1-800-864-4297
Fax 970-204-0761
www.cottonwoodpress.com